Whatever Happens to Little Women?

GENDER AND PRIMARY SCHOOLING

Edited by
Christine Skelton

Open University Press
Milton Keynes · Philadelphia

Open University Press
12 Cofferidge Close
Stony Stratford
Milton Keynes MK11 1BY

and
1900 Frost Road, Suite 101
Bristol, PA 19007, USA

First Published 1989

British Library Cataloguing in Publication Data

Whatever happens to little women? : gender and primary
    schooling. — (Gender and education)
    1. Great Britain. Schools. Sexism
    I. Skelton, Christine   II. Series
    370.19'345

    ISBN 0 335 09239 X (paper)

Library of Congress Cataloging-in-Publication Data

Whatever happens to little women? : gender and primary
    schooling / edited by Christine Skelton.
        p. cm. — (Gender and education series)
    Bibliography: p.
    Includes index.
    ISBN 0–335–09239–X
    1. Sex discrimination in education—England.   2. Sexism in
    education—England.   3. Education, Elementary—England.
    I. Skelton, Christine.   II. Series.
    LC212.83.G72E548   1989
    370.19'345—dc20

Typeset by Colset (Pte.) Limited, Singapore
Printed in Great Britain by Woolnough Bookbinding Limited
Irthlingborough, Northamptonshire

Contents

Series Editor's Introduction

During the life of this series, the extent of both research and policy interventions into gender and education has increased considerably, despite a political climate which is not especially favourable to such developments. Whereas in the past, much of the research was carried out solely by academics, recently more and more teachers have begun to do their own research. Partly as a result of this, there has been a much greater interchange between those in schools and those working in higher education. The fruitfulness of this is clearly reflected in this collection and in the personal biographies of its contributors. But this collection is also important for another reason. Comparatively little work has been done on the gender issues arising from primary education; much of the effort has gone into looking at secondary schooling. This book seeks to redress the balance by turning the spotlight firmly on gender and race/ethnicity issues in the primary school, exploring some of the problems, developments and initiatives taking place in that sector. The focus of the collection is, however, far from narrow, ranging over parents, pupils, teachers, curriculum, school organization, LEA policy and teacher education. The 1988 Education Act will have profound effects on all schools, but the introduction of the National Curriculum in particular is likely to fundamentally change the face of primary schooling. Other changes, such as greater governor control through Local Management of Schools (which will affect all primary schools through changes to how schools are funded, even though only larger primaries will actually gain budgetary autonomy) will put considerable pressure on the creative and innovative aspects of primary schooling. This book will be valuable in the struggle to retain the distinctiveness and wholeness of primary education, both by alerting us to the gender and race/ethnicity issues still to be addressed and by pointing out those positive developments which must be sustained, at a time when money and 'managerial efficiency' threaten to swallow schools' commitment to fulfilling teacher and pupil potential by eradicating social disadvantage.

Rosemary Deem

Notes on Contributors

Hilary Burgess is a senior lecturer in Primary Education at Westhill College, Birmingham.

Elizabeth Burn has been a primary school teacher in Gateshead and Newcastle for thirteen years. In 1986–7 she undertook a two-term fellowship at the University of Newcastle upon Tyne when she researched into children's toys and observed their use of Lego construction material.

Bruce Carrington worked in primary schools in London and is now a lecturer at the University of Newcastle upon Tyne. He has recently published an edited collection with Barry Troyna entitled *Children and Controversial Issues* (1988, Falmer) and a book written in conjunction with Geoffrey Short, *'Race' and the Primary School: Theory into Practice*, is due for publication in 1989 (NFER/Nelson).

John Gibbs is the headteacher of Houghton on the Hill CE Primary School and Evening Centre, Leicestershire. Prior to this, he was headteacher of Saltby CE Primary School, Melton Mowbray. He has taught in several schools in the Leicestershire area. In addition to his current post he is a course tutor for the Open University, Explaining Educational Issues course, and teaches courses on governing schools for the WEA.

Lesley Hart is the teacher adviser for Equal Opportunities (Gender) for Newcastle upon Tyne LEA. Before that she was head of English in an inner-city comprehensive school. She spent a year on a part-time secondment to Newcastle Polytechnic as Equal Opportunities Development Officer. Lesley Hart is a founder member of the Newcastle Sexism in Education Group and the Northern Network of Women Working on Equal Opportunities in Education. In 1986 she organized the workshops and activities for 2,000 schoolgirls at the Newcastle Women's Training Roadshow which was an event funded by the Women's National Committee.

Joy Rose was born in 1948. She has taught English in secondary schools in England, Canada and Sweden. She gave birth to two sons, Daniel who died from Sudden Infant Death Syndrome in 1982, and Joseph, now aged five. She became a deputy head-teacher in Manchester in 1985.

Geoffrey Short has extensive teaching experience in primary and middle schools and a long-standing interest in race and education. He is now a Lecturer in Education at Hatfield Polytechnic. His book written in conjunction with Bruce Carrington, *'Race' and the Primary School: Theory into Practice*, will be published by NFER/Nelson in 1989.

Christine Skelton is a lecturer in Education at the University of Newcastle upon Tyne. She taught in primary schools in Cleveland for several years before taking up a position as lecturer in the Early Years at Sunderland Polytechnic in 1985.

Barbara Thompson has been a primary school teacher for sixteen years. She has taught in the South, Midlands and North East regions of Britain. She obtained an MA in Women's Studies at the University of York in 1986 and is currently a tutor for the Open University teaching the MA in Gender and Education course.

Denise Trickett has taught for several years in Leeds primary schools. She is now Equal Opportunities support teacher for primary education, helping and advising teachers on equal opportunities and anti-sexist education. She is based at Elmete Primary Centre, Leeds.

Andrew Windass obtained a BA (Hons) from Durham University in 1975 and an MEd from the University of Newcastle upon Tyne in 1984. He is currently head of sociology at Ponteland County High School. In 1985–6 he undertook a secondment, sponsored by Northumberland TVEI, to investigate positive gender practice in Northumberland schools.

Acknowledgements

The contributors to this book would like to thank the following people: Kate Carr, Sue Dix, Elizabeth French, Tim Glanvill, Judy Hogg, Jackie Keating, Sheila Keating, Michael MacDonald, Pamela Martin, Lynne Ostle, Rebecca Ostle, Marcia Thompson, Eric Thompson, Christine Tompkins, Kath Wallace, and Sally Young.

I should like to thank the contributors for working so hard to complete their chapters against a background of job moves, illness and changes in personal circumstances. I would also like to thank my colleagues at Newcastle University; Carol Buswell, Bruce Carrington and Barry Troyna for their advice about editing; Stephen Munby for the discussions and the wine.

On a more personal level, I offer my grateful thanks to Mum, Dad, Trisha and, particularly, Alastair for their constant love and support.

Introduction

CHRISTINE SKELTON

Recognition of gender inequalities in primary education has only occurred in recent years. Following the Sex Discrimination Act (1975) research into gender and education tended to concentrate upon secondary schooling in an attempt to discover why girls and boys demonstrated clear differences in 'subject choice' at thirteen plus. The work of such people as Stanworth (1981), Whyld (1983) and Griffin (1985) made it evident that simply offering the same subjects to girls and boys could do nothing to alter the imbalance in 'option choice'. Rather, it was girls' exposure to gender discrimination in the 'hidden curriculum' which influenced their decisions and this process began much earlier than secondary schooling. As Whyte (1983a) points out:

> It is unlikely that these crucial differences between the sexes suddenly make their appearance at the age of 13. Their roots are to be uncovered in different patterns of growth in the primary years and in particular in the way that school prepares children for adult life. (Whyte 1983a: 8)

This book is not intended to reproduce the arguments represented elsewhere which identify how gender stereotyping pervades the primary years of education (Stones 1983; Hough 1985; French and French 1986). The aim is to provide an overall picture of gender stereotyping in the primary school from the perspective of parents, children and teachers, and to indicate how various LEAs (Local Education Authorities) have attempted to raise the profile of gender inequalities.

Before looking in detail at the content of the chapters in this book, one or two points need to be made to contextualize the contributions to this volume in the light of recent government changes and research into gender, 'race' and social class inequalities.

Gender inequalities, primary education and the National Curriculum

The contributors to this book write of their experiences at a time when a National Curriculum was little more than a gleam in the eye of the Secretary of State. Following the general election in June 1987, the mechanisms to introduce a National Curriculum in 1989 were rapidly put into operation and we have yet to discover what effects this will have on the commitment by LEAs to equal opportunities initiatives (see Chapters 8 and 9). Whilst the proposal documents for maths, science and English 5–11 failed to tackle adequately the issues surrounding equal opportunities, they did at least draw attention to this area. However, the final consultation reports provide dismal reading. The maths consultation report published in December 1988 leaves us in no doubt as to the importance accorded to equal opportunities. Only passing mention is made and that is to say 'These matters and others will form the bases for further work by Council and for circulars containing non-statutory guidance' (DES 1988: 13).

A similar situation exists for science. Kant (1987), writing about the National Curriculum 5–16 consultation document published in July 1987, suggests that a core curriculum based on maths, English and science in the primary years has the potential to provide girls with early experiences in science which would encourage them to pursue this subject in later years:

> Given the concern shown by HMI at the lack of scientific explora-
> tion in primary schools, this requirement may help those girls
> who are less likely to experience quasi-scientific and technical
> investigation in the course of childhood play. (p. 43)

The science proposal document published in August 1988 reinforced this by stating in its section 'Science for All' that 'particular attention needs to be given to the expectations and attitudes of girls at all stages . . .' (p. 91). But, in the same way that equal opportunities are skimmed over in the final maths report, the concern for girls' attitudes to science noted in the proposals is omitted from the final report. The message is

clear – 'Equal Opportunities' should be given little or no attention by schools in the implementation and practice of the
National Curriculum.

This attitude of the government comes as no surprise to those
of us who have been actively involved in promoting awareness
of gender inequalities in education. Acker (1986) refers to the
'vague support' of the DES (Department of Education and Science) towards equality in education and it appears that this
situation is set to continue if not worsen. It will be up to those
parents, teachers and LEAs committed to equal opportunities to
ensure that the implementation of the National Curriculum is
underpinned by a recognition of sexism, how it affects the
content of what is taught and an understanding of the complex
ways in which learning takes place.

Gender, 'race' and social class – recent research

The work carried out by, amongst others, Clarricoates (1978),
Hough (1983) and Swann and Graddol (1988) has shown how
gender stereotyping operates at a covert level within primary
education. More recent research argues that inequalities in
schooling cannot be neatly categorized into 'gender', 'race' or
'social class' (Wolpe 1988; Tizard *et al.* 1988). For example,
Tizard *et al.* (1988) suggest that a distorted picture of girls'
schooling emerges if gender is taken as the sole variable in
explaining females' educational experiences. As the authors say,
many studies have focused on ethnic groups and gender, and
considered their effects on school attainment rather than considering the interaction between these variables:

> Ethnic group, social class and sex are major status groups within
> our society. But each individual is a member not just of one
> group, but of all three. A child is not just a girl, but also, say,
> of Afro-Caribbean origin, and middle-class. Her outlook and
> experiences may be very different in many respects from those of
> a working-class boy of Afro-Caribbean origin, even though
> similar in other ways – notably, both are exposed to the racism
> in British society. (p. 22)

It is on this basis that a book of this kind, which concentrates
specifically on gender, and to a lesser extent on social class, can

be criticized. However, such a criticism would fail to take account of three factors which have influenced the research undertaken by the contributors to this book. As has been said, it is only very recently that recognition has been given to the interaction of gender, 'race' and social class variables on girls' schooling experiences. In the main, case studies have tended to concentrate on the 'underachievement' of particular groups: that is, girls, black students and working-class (boys) (Stanworth 1981; Wright 1987; Willis 1977). The chapters in this book have both continued this 'tradition' and been constrained in exploring interrelationships by a second factor, that of location. A perusal of the current literature suggests that the major impetus for change is occurring in the southern areas of Britain, and in particular the ILEA (Inner London Education Authority). It is because of the limited amount of published information regarding equal opportunities in primary education that the chapters in this book concentrate on work being carried out in the Midlands and Northern regions of Britain. These areas come under what Taylor (1988) has called the 'white highlands' – regions which are predominantly white and where the multicultural education debate has scarcely begun. This means that the work carried out by contributors in places such as Leicestershire, Northumberland, Newcastle upon Tyne and Leeds focuses on predominantly white school populations and therefore the writers have not been in a position to explore a range of school experiences, for example, those of black, middle-class girls.

A final factor is that of access to schools. Gender and 'race' inequalities in education are sensitive areas of investigation and many schools and LEAs are reluctant to engage with these issues. The reluctance to consider 'race' issues is even more marked in the 'white highlands' where the claim is often made that they have 'no problem here' (Gaine 1987). Consequently, some writers in this book have found themselves in a position where they have been unable to pursue lines of enquiry which would enable their findings to reflect gender, 'race' and social class variables.

It is clear that work needs to be carried out in the 'white highlands' which would provide some insight into the interrelationship of these three major social groupings in children's educational experiences. Since this information is not yet available, the suggestions given by the contributors may have to be modified or changed in the light of future research.

Contents

The book is divided into three sections. The first section, Parents, Children and Schools, examines perspectives on gender stereotyping from three different standpoints. In Chapter 1 Joy Rose offers a personal account of parental influence in encouraging a school to seriously consider inequality issues. The school Rose refers to is part of an 'Equal Opportunities' LEA but despite this several factors operate which conspire against gender and 'race' being placed high on the list of priorities, not least, the everyday constraints of teachers' classroom experiences, the hesitancy of many parents to 'interfere' in school policy and the lack of real, practical support from the LEA. The second chapter by Geoffrey Short and Bruce Carrington provides an interesting insight into the stereotypical perceptions children have of gender identities. This area is one which has been seriously neglected in studies of gender inequality in primary schooling. Drawing upon data from two schools, one predominantly working class the other predominantly middle class, they show how children's understanding of gender inequalities and other related issues may vary in accordance with age. It is their contention that unless direct teaching to challenge such perceptions makes a contrast with children's existing knowledge, it is unlikely to be effective. The final chapter in this section by Andrew Windass provides an overview of the gender-discriminatory practices which have been found in primary schooling. He undertook a project sponsored by Northumberland TVEI (Technical and Vocational Education Initiative) and highlights how and where gender discrimination occurs in children's schooling. His observations clearly demonstrate that gender discrimination, whilst not a part of the overt curriculum of primary schools, occupies a fundamental role in children's pre-school lives and in the educational experiences they receive at primary level.

The second section, Primary Teachers, considers the obstacles encountered in attempting to place gender on the agenda of primary schools and the career experiences of female teachers. In Chapter 4 I examine the ways in which gender can be an influential factor in the recruitment and 'training' (or, more appropriately, the 'professional socialization') of primary teachers. Barbara Thompson (Chapter 5) considers an issue which occurs in many of the chapters; that is, teacher attitudes towards gender inequalities in the primary school. On the basis of her own experience and research carried out with student primary teachers she argues that, in the main, teacher attitudes fall into two main categories – complacency and hostility. Thompson goes on to suggest how INSET courses can encourage teachers to reflect upon their attitudes towards gender issues and offers strategies whereby 'real' change may be achieved. In Chapter 6, Hilary Burgess adopts an autobiographical approach in discussing the careers of primary school women teachers. A particularly thought-provoking issue is that, for female primary teachers to be successful, they have to 'know their place': that is, they should be prepared to accept the status quo because attempts to 'better oneself' by taking higher degrees can actually inhibit their chances of career promotion. Lesley Hart, an Equal Opportunities Advisory Teacher, looks at women headteachers' perceptions of themselves and how they are treated by others (Chapter 7). Her findings emphasize the isolation of a headteacher's role, at the same time identifying the ways in which this situation is exacerbated for female headteachers.

The third section, Policy and Practice, examines LEA policy and how such policies affect the classroom situation. John Gibbs (Chapter 8) and Denise Trickett (Chapter 9) demonstrate the ways in which Leicestershire and Leeds have sought to address and redress gender inequalities in primary schooling.

Before considering the contents of these chapters in more detail a question which should be answered is: why is there such a wide variation in LEAs' responses to gender policy-making? The answer is that following the Sex Discrimination Act (1975) the DES placed responsibility for ensuring the tenets of the Act were adhered to on the shoulders of LEAs – the DES itself was to occupy an 'advisory role'. Passing responsibility for implementing the Sex Discrimination Act to LEAs explains why individual authorities have approached the issue in a variety of ways. Some LEAs have policy statements which have been implemented and are monitored, others have statements which reside at the back of the filing cabinet, and others have failed to recognize that gender discrimination is an element which needs to be addressed. The guidance sent out by the DES informed LEAs that their obligation should be seen in the light of ensuring equal *access* to girls and boys to the same curriculum. The emphasis placed on curriculum *subjects* inferred that any gender discrimination in schools could be rectified by providing girls and boys with the opportunity to undertake the same courses of study. Of course this guidance side-stepped any concern for the wider implications of sex-role stereotyping found in the 'hidden curriculum'. This resulted in what Gibbs and Trickett refer to as an *ad hoc* approach to gender equality by their LEAs.

Another factor worth noting is that both chapters concerned with LEA initiatives place emphasis on 'Equal Opportunities' rather than 'anti-sexist' initiatives. Weiner (1985) has neatly summarized the distinguishing features of these approaches. A simplistic explanation is that 'Equal Opportunity' initiatives denote a concern for ensuring that girls get an equal share of the educational 'cake' as it exists – that is, the same number of girls opting for science subjects as boys – with a view to more women entering traditional male areas of the labour market and obtaining positions of authority. Supporters of 'anti-sexist' initiatives place emphasis on changing the educational 'cake' – that is, recognizing women's contributions to society, their values and attitudes – and, most importantly, stresses the promotion of a female-based confidence and motivation (see Weiner 1985, 1986). The main point here, however, is that:

> Whereas [Equal Opportunities supporters] fail to address the relationship between patriarchy, power and women's subordination, the [anti-sexist supporters] place it at the centre of their thinking. (Weiner 1985: 9)

These lines of thought are not disparate and 'Equal Opportunities' can be seen as a 'way in' for supporters of anti-sexist initiatives. Weiner (1986) has said that the two approaches are not discrete, as anti-sexist, or:

> . . . girl-centred education [is] not necessarily an alternative to egalitarian strategies but [is] a much more powerful dimension and extension to their work. (p. 273)

Given that any consideration of gender issues in education is regarded as a 'political minefield' (see Chapter 9), it is not surprising to find that LEA initiatives reported in section three of this book have leaned towards 'Equal Opportunities' rather than 'anti-sexist' approaches.

In the cases of both Leicestershire and Leeds, a specific policy for tackling gender discrimination within primary education did not exist. Gibbs notes how Leicestershire's approach was a 'bottom-up' strategy. Work was carried out in individual schools and, as he suggests, gender inequalities were considered in a variety of ways. His chapter provides valuable information regarding practical strategies schools/teachers can adopt. In a slightly different vein, Denise Trickett in Chapter 9 considers the 'top-down' policy adopted by Leeds LEA. Whilst Leeds, at that time, did not have a specific 'Equal Educational Opportunities' statement, it did have a general Equal Opportunities Council Policy which was applied to education. The emphasis here is more toward a central initiative but, as with Gibbs's chapter, highlights the strategies which can be adopted.

The final chapter by Elizabeth Burn explores how her involvement with Newcastle's Sexism in Education Group affected her own classroom practices. She stresses the importance of teachers undertaking research into gender inequalities in their own classrooms. Her experience of carrying out a toy survey and observing children's use of Lego was useful, not least because it shed light on children's 'gendered play' but also because it generated an awareness of how societal expectations of 'women's role' and 'primary teaching' affects the self-perception of many female teachers.

Reading or 'dipping into' the contents of this book is unlikely to provide any blueprints for an ultimate solution to 'the way forward' regarding gender discrimination in the primary school. What it does do is indicate some of the strategies which have, and can be, adopted in order to put gender on the agenda of primary schooling. Whether it be 'equal opportunity' initiatives in themselves or equal opportunities with a view to anti-sexist education, the 'problems' of gender issues within primary education are beginning to be heard.

Parents, Children and Schools

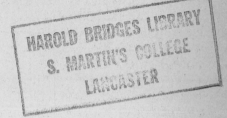

CHAPTER 1

A Parent's Voice

JOY ROSE

School playgrounds are tough places for 5 year olds. Most parents that I have met feel trepidation at the thought of their child being thrust into this situation. All important to the child is to be like everyone else, to be accepted. There lies the dilemma for the parent who wants her son to be different from the stereotypical male norm. What do I want my son to be? I want him to be sensitive; to appreciate beauty in the natural world and the world of the arts; to be gentle and caring; to be able to express love; to respect women; to be aware of the contribution of women in all aspects of life; to value work traditionally done by women; to be adventurous and unafraid; to be independent; to feel secure and unthreatened; to be happy as himself. I would want these things for a daughter too but the emphasis might be different. Whilst I also want my son to be strong and have high aspirations, for a daughter these would be first on the list.

How easy is it for a boy to develop in these directions? Can a school facilitate such developments? As a secondary teacher of eighteen years' experience I am fully aware of the way in which schools can be brutalizing as a result of institutional structures, despite the campaigning work being done by many individual educationalists and a few education authorities to change this. As a feminist committed to striving for a more equal society it was not surprising that the prospect of my child starting school a year ago filled me with well-intentioned zeal aimed at challenging the traditional educational values of the local primary school. I believe that the school and parents should work in partnership to ensure an educational experience that challenges stereotyping and allows a child to develop into an adult undamaged by sexist expectations of her or him. However, at the end of my child's first year of schooling I have discovered how difficult it is to establish that partnership, how slow the process is, and that any influence I have as a parent will be for the benefit of children in the future rather than directly affecting my own child.

The local education authority

Manchester City Council is an 'Equal Opportunities Employer'. Within Manchester Education Committee there have been many anti-sexist initiatives, some of which I have been involved in. Two female Senior District Inspectors have taken on, as part of their work, responsibility for equal opportunities in gender. Several inspectors are clearly aware of the issues as related to their subject specialism. Developments in this field, however, have been *ad hoc* and rely upon individual evangelism. The LEA has recently appointed an inspector with responsibility for Equal Opportunities and given him a two-year secondment to prepare for the work involved. Whilst this is indeed a move forward, there are many women in the city who already have the expertise and who could have begun the work immediately, though this would have required a promotion to give one of these women sufficient status to have an impact.

My first task was to write to the CEO (Chief Education Officer) to ask for copies of the following (if they existed):

1 a written statement of policy
2 guidelines for headteachers
3 advisers/inspectors with a major responsibility for anti-sexist strategies
4 funding allocated to primary schools for anti-sexist initiatives
5 in-service arrangements for headteachers, advisers, inspectors on gender issues
6 guidelines for class teachers

I did not receive a reply from the CEO. Whilst it was unlikely that such documents existed, I hoped my letter might prompt recognition of an omission that needed rectifying. My letter, written later in the year to the Senior Inspector with responsibility for primary education, did receive a response. The reply included the sentence, 'As you know issues related to the development of equal opportunities are a high priority in the authority and there is no doubt that we would wish to support your developmental work in this area.' He contacted the school to ensure the headteacher knew I had his support, which opened the door for me.

Choosing a school

There were two primary schools available to my child close to my home, each with a very different character. One has a reputation for being progressive and is attended predominantly by children from white, middle-class families, many of whom are aware of and committed to anti-sexist education. The other school has a reputation for using more traditional classroom methods but has an intake which is more mixed in terms of race and class. Both schools have male headteachers whose answers to questions about equal opportunity policies were tokenistic and superficial. For example, 'We support equal opportunities principles here but, of course, we can't afford to replace all our books at once' and, 'Of course we believe in equal opportunities and Miss (name) keeps me in line'. I chose the latter school because of the mixed intake of children. It was fortunate that the infant and junior departments operate as two separate schools as I found the headteacher of the infant department to be a strong, successful woman. In my later interviews with parents, the headteacher was frequently mentioned as providing a positive role model for daughters.

The infant school has an excellent academic reputation. I am impressed by the well-organized classrooms, the bright, lively displays and the class teacher's sensitivity to my child's individual academic needs. The teachers cope efficiently with large classes and insufficient space in a Victorian building with a flagged playground surrounded by iron railings with major roads on two sides but a park on the other two. Nevertheless, the building is light, bright and cheerful and the atmosphere is one of harmonious learning. My child has enjoyed his first year at school. I would like it to be more progressive and flexible but in reality I have few criticisms, at this stage, other than gender stereotyping.

Some gender issues in the first year

When I had raised the subject of anti-sexist strategies at my
preliminary visit I realized that this was a very low priority and
my later observations confirmed this initial view. My first major
concern was a Christmas display which filled the walls of an
entire corridor. It was a superb presentation of children's work
from all age groups and most children had contributed something to it. The display linked up with the curriculum work and
with a Christmas visit to the theatre. Why was I concerned? The
theme was Snow White, a popular fairy story, play and cartoon
much loved by children. However, through this medium,
damaging racist and sexist attitudes were being conveyed. Snow
White's virtues are her white skin, her beauty and her efficient
housekeeping! The story was presented in a frieze of scenes:

- Snow White hated by her jealous stepmother – reflecting
  female vanity and selfishness;
- Snow White lured to the forest to an intended death by a
  calculating, ruthless female but saved by a gentle, humble
  male unable to commit this act;
- Snow White shocked at the dwarfs' untidy home – female
  domesticity innate even in a princess;
- Snow White loved and admired by men – no female friend-
  ships;
- Snow White foolishly tricked by the scheming stepmother –
  female lack of wisdom;
- Snow White rescued by a handsome prince!

My child took me to view this display several times. He gazed
enraptured by it, transported into realms of romance and wonder. As we followed the story along the corridor I made my usual
adaptations:

- Snow White the source of envy because of her cleverness and
  kindness;
- Snow White bored by household chores in the dwarfs' house
  and missing her friends.

These adaptations in no way interfered with my child's pleasure,
but mitigated the damage.
　I discussed this display with several parents to assess the

support I had and found a range of responses. My concerns were shared by all I spoke to. How does a black or Asian girl relate to this story? What is the reaction of a white girl whose mother would have her aspire to more than marriage and housework? How does a boy learn to value a female partner for intellectual and personal attributes other than appearance? The way of dealing with the issues was less unanimous. Several parents felt that interference with our traditional heritage of fairy stories was wrong. Instead a balance could be achieved by a study of folk tales from other cultures, by ensuring that alternative role models were provided in other aspects of the curriculum. Parents doubted, however, that this actually happened. Another approach suggested by a parent was presenting the tale unedited but creating opportunities to discuss the issues. Do you think it was much fun staying at home all day cleaning the house for the dwarfs? If you were Snow White what would you prefer to do? All the children I asked would much rather go down the diamond mines. One 6 year old suggested that if the dwarfs did some housework each, as her daddy did, then Snow White would have lots of time to spend in the diamond mines.

Within six months of starting school my child had abandoned the term 'fire fighter' for 'fireman'. He told me that I was not capable of rescuing him in play, as women had not got any muscles, despite a diet of 'right on' fiction at home, plus a compromise by reading 'Shera, Princess of Power', who frequently saves the day and no one kicks sand in her face! I can no longer be referred to as Dr Rose when administering sticking plaster but am henceforth to be addressed as 'nurse', despite the presence of a female general practitioner at our local health centre. I am quite sure the school does not promulgate these invidious inaccuracies. No doubt media and peer-group influence is far greater. The ideal would be the school and parents working together to combat such distortions of reality. Having perceived a problem, how do we address it? I made special arrangements to leave work early to have a discussion with the teacher. But, at the end of the day, she was always surrounded by parents with specific concerns about their offspring. A quick glance at the queue, the photograph money to be collected, the pictures to be mounted, the part-finished wall display, the books awaiting marking, the equipment to be tidied and the work to be prepared for the next day and no wonder my tentative comments

received a weary reply. The teacher needs appreciation at this
time of day not criticism, however constructive.

Perhaps because I spoke mainly to middle-class parents, some
with professional training, there was a strong faith in the home
values being deep and it was felt that discussions at home about
apparent contradictions could restore the balance. Several parents preferred to challenge at home any prejudicial attitudes
which emerged at school. Two specific gender issues were raised
by parents. A minor issue was the letter sent out each year
requesting that all girls, as opposed to children with long hair,
wear bathing caps for the weekly swimming lesson. It was felt
that boys with long hair should wear bathing caps as well and
girls with short hair should not need to. The parents' response
had been to ignore the request rather than challenge it outright.
Another issue dating from a few years ago concerned an objection to segregated playgrounds. Several parents of girls were
involved, but also parents of boys who felt that the male playground did not offer a sufficient range of activities for boys who
did not wish to play football. The parents' views were heard but
no action was taken. Only a change of headteacher, when the
original one retired, produced action.

Other parents

The parents I spoke to reflected or expanded upon my own
experience, as is inevitable. It was a small number of parents with
whom I came into contact or who were referred to me by those I
already knew. I did not seek out those with widely differing
views. Nevertheless, the parents I spoke to are typical of a wider
group and indicate a body of support for change. Their image
was of a conventional school. They were not overwhelmingly
dissatisfied by this but would prefer it to be more progressive
and would support a lobby led by someone else! They felt that
teaching staff had some awareness of gender and race issues, but
doubted this had led to any significant modification of attitudes
or that the curriculum had been influenced in more than a
minimal way. It was felt that action or inaction on gender or race
was left to individual teachers rather than being enforced
through a school policy. Different attitudes prevailed in each
classroom. Parents who were teachers were much more critical
than parents with other occupations who had a deferential

respect for the 'experts' and a reluctance to interfere directly, though they would support a lobby for change. Over the past ten years parents had seen changes. Some terminology had been officially outlawed such as 'Wendy House' being replaced by 'play house'. A few years ago when painting self-portraits Asian children had painted themselves pink because brown paint had not been made available. This no longer occurred. There was clearly an increase in daily involvement of parents in the classroom. Some parents went in regularly to run the home library, or assist with computers. Several parents voiced willingness to share their skills and expertise, but felt the need to be invited to do so. Some parents had been into classrooms to talk about aspects of their own culture. Another concern expressed was the need for parents to be kept fully informed. On one occasion parents had grumbled in the playground and voiced their opinions to the parents' committee who presented these views to the headteacher. Action was out of the head's control, but a letter was sent to all parents explaining the situation. This in itself was regarded as progress, recognizing that parental opinion is important and that we are entitled to information. Increased opportunity for contact with governors, copies of the agendas for governors' meetings and reports from those meetings were all considered to be desirable for parents.

My discussions with other parents about their perception of their power to effect change revealed a range of views. It was felt that a parent had to earn credibility with the staff. Having had several children succeed in the school was one way. An academically successful child does not threaten the system. Being in a professional occupation was deemed useful. The view was voiced that there was a class division of parental involvement and that middle-class and professional parents felt less threatened by schools, though even they were cautious. Becoming involved as a governor or member of the parent associations lent authority to a parent's voice. Obviously regular attendance at events, social occasions, meetings is essential. Being prepared to be patient, to recognize that you could be a threat at first and working beyond that initial reaction led eventually to an amenable response from the teaching staff.

For most parents the immediate happiness of their child was the highest priority and it was difficult to tackle issues with a view to the future. Most parents felt very welcome to discuss personal problems related to their own child, but that they would tread very gingerly on any wider issues, afraid that the experts would resent the intrusion. If they felt strongly about an issue they would approach the class teacher first, but would find approaching a headteacher somewhat daunting. Involving a parent governor would be the next stage and the LEA would be the last resort. Most parents who were not actively involved did not realize that the association of friends of the school was more than a fund-raising body. I listened to articulate, educated and confident parents who were aware of, and concerned about, gender and race in schools and almost all of them believed that it was the responsibility of the LEA to ensure balance in the curriculum. Aware of the heavy burden carried by primary school teachers, it was suggested that additional teachers should be appointed to promote change, and that the LEA had an obligation to facilitate progress.

Where we are now

On visits to the school as a parent, the headteacher has always been most charming and the class teacher helpful and frank. The day I spent in my child's school was, indeed, very enlightening and enjoyable. The headteacher had been reluctant to approve this request and made clear that gender issues were not a high priority although she emphasized that all children were treated equally. Despite this, on the actual day, she made me very welcome, gave up a great deal of her time and allowed me complete freedom. I saw a delightful assembly on flowers, involving the children. I was pleased to see that there did not appear to be preconceived attitudes amongst the boys who were keen to identify names, although only one girl was called to answer. Children were not segregated according to gender, sat together, lined up together and, in the classrooms, appeared to be receiving equal attention. At break and lunchtime girls and boys played happily together and ate together. Skipping ropes were issued to girls and boys alike. 'Link Up' reading scheme had replaced 'Ladybird'; this was an LEA initiative. Even this replacement reading scheme lacked positive role models and used sexist language at times. Within the school building there were examples of women in authority but there were no adult males. This was perhaps less disconcerting than the common pattern of a male appointed as teacher and rapidly being promoted over the female teachers!

My one serious concern was the categorization of children according to gender. This occurred overtly after breaktime. I was warned that I was going to see some 'sexist behaviour' by one teacher but this was justified on the grounds of practicality. Children were asked to form a line of boys and a line of girls to use the toilets. In the same family both genders share a toilet but in schools this is not acceptable even though the urinals have been removed. However, the separate lines are less damaging than the competition being promoted between the sexes, for example, asking for the straightest or quietest line. This is distressing to me as the parent of a boy. At present he does not distinguish between girls' and boys' toys, games and company and he has not absorbed the macho attitudes prevalent in society. He does not exhibit the contempt for, or embarrassment with, girls which, of course, may occur as he gets older. As he actually prefers skipping to football he often chooses to play with girls. I like him as he is. If, however, he finds that a distinction is being observed around him, that he is expected to compete with girls and be better than them, that they are considered to be 'cissy' and their games unsuitable for boys, I may find I have a lonely and unhappy son. Such categorizations can be very difficult to overcome. It occurred in pockets throughout the school. Teachers who said they saw all children as the same were actually distinguishing and referring to children by gender without appearing to realize it: 'You two boys, please sit down', 'Will you three girls stop chattering!', 'I can see one boy sitting up very nicely', 'The girls are ready, why aren't the boys?' I did see at least one lesson where this did not occur at all. This took place in a games lesson where children were racing, boys and girls in the same races. Coming 'first' was ignored and other aspects of their performance were commented upon by the teacher. It was clear that all the class, including a physically handicapped child, athletic or otherwise, were thoroughly enjoying this activity and gender was irrelevant.

It is this issue of categorization of children by gender that I wish to raise with the headteacher and governors next term. However, this is more complex than the head, if she agrees to the proposal, simply making a statement of policy for the school.

Seperate boys

There is a desperate need for the teachers to meet to discuss the problem and for awareness to be raised amongst the staff that it is indeed a problem. My observations have highlighted for me the disproportionate allocation of resources between primary and secondary schools, the lack of opportunity for staff meetings, insufficient or inadequate reprographic and technological equipment, shortage of clerical assistance, shortage of materials, too large classes, lack of space and insufficient ancillary staffing. Teachers were working all day, throughout their lunchtime and after school. They had evidently produced many of their materials themselves at home. How can such teachers find time to reflect, to meet and discuss? If the resource implications of the primary school situation are not addressed by the LEA then it is inevitable that gender issues will remain on the educational fringe.

Structures already in existence to influence change

If a parent wishes to influence the educational policy of a school there are many formal and informal structures through which one can work. A grievance can be aired or concern raised by speaking to the class teacher informally after school, although the immense difficulties already referred to make this only useful as a starting point. An appointment with the headteacher is also possible but this is fraught with obstacles. Is it possible for a parent to have time off work? How comfortable are parents in schools? Probably, apart from parents who are teachers or in professional occupations, most of us feel threatened by the school institution. Do parents have credibility with the professionals? Do parents understand the complexities and obstacles in the way of change? Headteachers are very busy and can feel threatened, especially if parents only seem to complain or criticize. Headteachers may not appreciate the significance of a parent's concern or they may find that their attempts to implement change are blocked by their staff, by lack of time to meet as a staff, or by lack of resources.

Parent governors exist to represent parents' views at governors' meetings. The governing body is becoming increasingly powerful with greater parental representation now than ever before. The effectiveness of this route depends on the way in which parental concern is received and reported by the governor at the meeting. The Annual Governors' Report to parents is a very important meeting to attend in order to raise issues and also to begin becoming involved. Here, parents can indicate that they are committed to the school and not simply to one issue and can raise an issue in the hearing of other parents. Parental presence at such meetings lends support to other parents and the parent governors.

Social occasions run by the school are not entirely aimed at fundraising but are also attempts to reduce the barriers by offering contact in an informal setting. They are not the place to launch into a major issue but they do open doors to communication with teachers and other parents. Another important opportunity to establish a channel of communication is the time spent standing in the playground whilst collecting children. I found this was regarded as a very valuable and useful network to ascertain whether particular concern was felt by other parents and to rally support. Schools could consider offering a room at this time for parents to meet each other and teacher representatives on occasions. Unfortunately this network is not available to employed parents who have to arrange childcare. A childminder who was also a parent of another child in the school acted as a contact into this network.

The LEA and inspectorate can be drawn into debate about educational issues in schools although there is a danger of creating hostility between parent and school. My requests for information from the LEA drew no response. I did seek and achieve inspectorate approval for a day's observation in my son's school. My letter included a complimentary paragraph commenting upon positive aspects of the school which, as I had chosen to send my son there, were quite true. It resulted in replies to the headteacher and myself, from the inspector, which no doubt lent weight to my request.

Most schools run a Parent Teacher Association or similar group. In my case, the school runs an association of friends of the school, not necessarily parents, and not teachers. This was set up by the headteacher of the junior school, initially as a group of interested people, but they are now an elected body. It is more than a fundraising group and it addresses social and curriculum issues. The establishment of this group has opened the door tentatively to parents, who have been given time, reprographic facilities and a space in which to meet and talk.

CHAPTER 2

Discourse on Gender: The Perceptions of Children Aged Between Six and Eleven

GEOFFREY SHORT AND BRUCE CARRINGTON

There is no shortage of policy documents and guidelines currently available to teachers outlining strategies to obviate gender inequality in schools (See Chapters 8 and 9, this book). Yet despite the burgeoning body of literature suggesting how, for example, sexist attitudes and behaviour among pupils might be challenged, such interventions generally take little or no account of age or social class differences in children's understanding of the issues involved.

If there is any readily discernible leitmotif underpinning this chapter, it can best be summarized by the following dictum:

> if we do not know the nature of children's thinking about society,
> it is difficult to plan appropriate learning contexts for them.
> (Campbell and Lawton 1970: 904)

In so far as unfair treatment is central to any discussion of sexism, it follows that anti-sexist initiatives ought to be informed by what we know of age-related differences in children's knowledge of such treatment. It is also important to know how children at different ages explain gender inequality (for, clearly, their explanations, and the myths and half-truths that masquerade as explanations, will determine their perception of inequality as fair or otherwise).

Extant literature provides us with very little upon which to base a successful anti-sexist initiative. We know that most children can label themselves correctly as a boy or girl by the age of 3 (e.g. Fagot 1985), and that they usually acquire the concept of gender stability – the notion that gender remains fixed throughout life – within a year or two of acquiring the concept of gender identity (e.g. Slabey and Frey 1975). We also know that true gender constancy tends to emerge between the ages of 6 and 7, marking the child's recognition that the sex of an individual is unaffected by perceptual transformations such as changes in hairstyle and clothing (e.g. Kohlberg 1966).

Research has not only uncovered the chronology of gender identity, stability and constancy, it has also revealed the extent and nature of sex role stereotyping throughout the years of early and middle childhood. The research has taken three forms: the first and most direct involves presenting children with a number of stereotypical statements and then asking which of two representative figures (one male, the other female) is the more likely to have made or acted in accordance with the statement (e.g. Best *et al.* 1977). Such studies, however, are both methodologically unsound and ethically dubious. One methodological weakness stems from providing children with a forced choice. They must select either the male or the female figure and cannot respond in such a way as to suggest that a given statement might apply equally to both figures or to neither. In Best's study, for example, 'the examiner insisted upon a definite response to each story; if the subject hesitated, the examiner told him [*sic*] to "try one" or to "point to one of them" ' (p. 1377). Had the children in this and similar investigations been given more than an either/or option, the results might have been quite different. Even where children have been given the opportunity to express their indifference or neutrality on gender issues (e.g. Meyer 1980), the studies suffer from not allowing the children to discuss what they know but are not asked. Such data may, therefore, present a partial and distorted account of children's understanding of sex role stereotyping. From an ethical point of view, the major concern with forced and extended choice designs is that they may either reinforce prevailing and often negative stereotypes of both sexes or introduce such stereotypes to children who were previously unaware of them.

The second approach to studying the development of sex role stereotypes is through observation of children's behaviour either in natural settings or in the laboratory. The assumption here is that when children choose, for example, to play with stereotyped toys or to wear gender-appropriate clothes, they are cognizant of a cultural stereotype.

A third means of investigating developmental changes in stereotyping is associated with William Damon (1977). His approach was to read a story about a boy with cross-sex toy preferences and then follow it up with a discussion of related moral issues in the form of a semi-structured interview.

Despite their different emphases, these three approaches leave us in no doubt that children from a very early age are aware of cultural norms in relation to gender. However, we have no data on *why* children think that certain types of behaviour or possession are appropriate for one sex but inappropriate for the other. Nor do we have any data on the forms of gender differentiation that children at different ages regard as unfair. Moreover, much of the available research is not only American but has been undertaken with children between the ages of 3 and 6. Of the 1,600 investigations reviewed by Macoby and Jacklin (1974), for example, more than three-quarters were conducted within this age range.

Children's understanding of gender differentiation: an ethnographic study

To redress the balance, we draw upon ethnographic data derived from semi-structured interviews with 161 children attending two 'all-white' schools in the south of England: 'Workington Primary' and 'Middleton Primary'. The sample comprised: 56 top infants (aged 6 and 7); 50 second-year juniors (aged 8 and 9); and 55 fourth-year juniors (aged 10 and 11). Workington Primary was situated in the heart of a council estate and had a predominantly working-class catchment. Middleton Primary, in contrast, had a largely middle-class clientele living in spacious detached and semi-detached dwellings.

The fieldwork was undertaken by Geoffrey Short between February and October 1987. Having established some rapport with the children in their classrooms, he then invited each child to select a friend who would accompany them 'to look at and talk about some pictures'. (The overwhelming majority of the pupils were interviewed in pairs.) There were three sets of pictures altogether, each telling a 'story': one about gender relations, another about 'race' and a third about class. In this chapter, we are primarily concerned to examine the children's understanding of gender differentiation. (N.B. Their responses to the remaining issues are discussed in Carrington and Short 1989.)

The first of the three pictures on gender deliberately reversed the active-male/passive-female stereotype, for it depicted a woman driving a car with a man as passenger. Traditional sex roles were challenged further in the second picture showing the car having broken down, the woman fixing it and the man, a mere spectator. Finally, in the third picture, the couple were seen driving away.

Awareness of gender stereotypes

Having been shown the three pictures, the children were asked to describe what was happening. Those who failed to comment spontaneously on the counter-stereotypical behaviour of the man and the woman in the second picture were asked if there was anything unusual in the story. (It was stressed that 'unusual' meant something that doesn't normally happen, not something that was in any way 'wrong'.) As can be seen from Table 2.1, a substantial proportion of top infants (especially at Middleton) only referred to the sex role reversal in response to some form of prompt, such as: 'Can you see anything else unusual?' Both the second- and the fourth-year juniors at Workington were in absolutely no doubt as to what was 'amiss'; at Middleton, this was true only of the 10 and 11 year olds. (N.B. The data in all the tables below show the *number of pairs* who referred to a particular category on *at least one occasion* during interview. The tables also show the total number of pairs (N) in each age group who were asked the question.)

The children were asked next why it is that men rather than women usually repair cars. As Table 2.2 makes clear, the most common 'explanations' in all year groups at both schools were that men are stronger, more knowledgeable and less concerned with their appearance.

Among the youngest children there seemed to be a strong feeling that this particular stereotype inevitably resulted from either the inherent properties of men and women or from some pre-ordained division of labour according to gender:

Table 2.1

Middleton	6/7 year olds	8/9 year olds	10/11 year olds
Cognizant of stereotype:			
With prompting	6	3	0
Without prompting	8	12	16
Not cognizant	1	0	0
N =	15	15	16*
Workington			
With prompting	2	0	0
Without prompting	11	10	11
Not cognizant	0	0	0
N =	13	10	11

*Because there was an odd number of 10/11 year olds at Middleton, one child was interviewed by himself. His responses have been excluded from the data presented in this chapter.

Table 2.2 Why do men normally mend cars?

Middleton	6/7 year olds	8/9 year olds	10/11 year olds
Physical attributes – stronger	2	8	3
Men get dirty/less concerned with their appearance	6	6	8
Men are less ignorant/more competent	7	9	3
Women do other things	3	1	3
Men drive cars/work more with mechanical things	3	2	0
Stereotype (i.e. social norms)	0	3	6
Personality (e.g. men are more interested in mechanical things)	1	3	1
Tautology/other	4	3	1
N =	15	15	9

Workington			
Physical attributes – stronger	10	3	5
Men get dirty/less concerned with their appearance	4	5	4
Men are less ignorant/more competent	7	7	7
Women do other things	3	3	2
Men drive cars/work more with mechanical things	0	4	2
Stereotype (i.e. social norms)	2	0	2
Personality	1	1	0
Tautology/other	2	0	0
N =	13	10	11

GS: Why do men tend to fix cars?

Michelle (6 years, 7 months): Because women aren't very good at it.

GS: Why aren't they?

Michelle: 'Cos they aren't strong enough and can't do it properly.

Lisa (6 years, 7 months): Because women like to be tidy and men don't mind.

Stuart (7 years, 1 month): 'Cos women do other things like cooking and men like fixing things.

Essentially, the infants thought the world of work had to be as it is and could not be otherwise:

Christopher: (6 years, 7 months) Men are *supposed* to (mend cars) because they're clever and women are *supposed* to do the cooking.

GS: Do you think that women can mend cars as well as men?

Dominic: (6 years, 8 months) No.

GS: Why not?

Dominic: 'Cos they don't know what it's all about.

GS: Why don't they know?

Dominic: 'Cos God made them like that.

There was some evidence of a small minority of second-year juniors appreciating that men and women's role in the occupational structure is not inevitable. They seemed aware that things could be different, but were either at a loss to know why traditional work patterns persisted or offered an unconvincing (and somewhat idiosyncratic) explanation:

Emma: (9 years, 10 months) If women [repaired cars] they might get it wrong.
Natalie: (9 years, 0 months) But if they were taught they wouldn't get it wrong.
GS: Why aren't women taught to do it?
Natalie: Don't know.

Matthew (9 years, 6 months), having agreed that women could be as competent as men at mending cars, was then asked why men and women in general tended to have different occupations. (Other responses to this latter question are recorded in Table 2.3.)

Matthew: 'Cos men like men's jobs and women like women's jobs.
GS: But why?
Matthew: 'Cos men learnt about the jobs at college when women didn't.
GS: Why don't women go to college to learn certain jobs?
Matthew: 'Cos girls aren't bothered to do it. They just want to go out every night.

References amongst the 10 and 11 year olds to physical strength suggest that some of them, in common with younger children, see the relationship between car repair and gender as biologically determined. However, the number of such children who referred to stereotypes, and specifically to the role of upbringing, points to a greater realization among the fourth-year juniors that employment prospects are not determined at conception.

When the top infants and second-year juniors commented on the existence of stereotypes, they did so without making reference to the power of expectations. They assumed that stereotypes were based on some underlying and fundamental difference between men and women and that this difference, rather than the stereotype itself, accounted for the distinctive behaviour of the two sexes. For example, when Adam (a second year) was asked why it is that men normally repair cars, he replied: 'Men do that kind of job.' When asked why women do not do it, he said, 'Because they don't like to get themselves dirty.' Among the fourth years there *seemed* to be a greater recognition that stereotypes might influence behaviour quite independently. For example, Andrea remarked: 'People just assume that it's men all the time,' and Laurence said, 'Women weren't brought up to do the technical stuff.' Whilst both these comments imply that women have as much ability as men to mend cars, it should be noted that no fourth year was insistent that stereotypes, by themselves, could determine behaviour. Thus, Laurence raised no objection when his friend spoke about men repairing cars because of their greater strength, nor did Andrea demur at her partner's suggestion that 'women don't like getting dirty'.

Having explained why men rather than women tend to mend cars, the children were asked if they could provide further examples of jobs more often associated with one sex than the other and then account for this pattern of employment. Compared with the previous question relating to car repair, the latter part of this second question was both more abstract and more general. It is thus not surprising that the youngest children at Workington, who *may* have been considerably less able academically than their Middleton counterparts, (cf. Hughes 1986) seemed to find it especially hard to offer an explanation.

Livesley and Bromley (1973) noted a marked increase in the use of 'central statements' (i.e. those referring to personality) between the ages of 7 and 8. They further observed that such statements became increasingly prominent in the descriptions of individuals given by children between the ages of 8 and 15. The data in Table 2.3 partially confirms Livesley and Bromley's claim in that the proportion of 8/9-year-old pairs who commented on personality was considerably higher than the proportion of 6/7-year-old pairs (9/25 as compared with 2/14). However, in view of the small number of fourth-year juniors as compared with second years who referred to specific personality traits, the data suggest that the developmental progression proposed by Livesley and Bromley might not apply when children are asked to explain why people behave in a particular way. (Among the fourth years who did talk about personality, one described women as 'more gentle', another as 'more careful' and a third, Kelley (11 years, 6 months), when asked why she said women were better at housework replied: 'Cos they can get on with it and men get bored more easily'.)

In so far as these data conflict with Livesley and Bromley's findings, the contradiction can most easily be resolved by assuming that children aged 7 and above generally have the

Table 2.3 Why do there seem to be some jobs for men and some jobs for women?

Middleton	6/7 year olds	8/9 year olds	10/11 year olds
Differential talents	1	3	1
Stereotype (social norms)	1	2	2
Physical attributes (e.g. strength)	1	5	7
Lack of opportunity/ training	1	2	0
Personality differences	2	6	2
Differences in knowledge/ competence	2	2	2
Differing concern over appearance	0	0	4
Differential power of men and women	0	0	3
Don't know/tautology/ other	3	3	0
	N = 8	15	10

Workington			
Differential talents	0	2	2
Stereotype (social norms)	0	2	2
Physical attributes (e.g. strength)	1	5	4
Personality differences	0	3	1
Differences in knowledge/ competence	0	2	0
Differing concern over appearance	0	2	1
Mutual convenience	0	1	0
Necessary for fairness/ equality	0	0	2
Don't know/tautology/ other	6	2	1
	N = 6	10	9

ability to conceptualize individuals and groups in terms of personality traits, but will only make use of this ability when they deem it appropriate. As far as their perception of gender and the world of work is concerned, older children seem to attach

more importance to factors such as physical strength and concern with appearance when explaining why men and women
tend to perform different roles. Some Middleton fourth years,
though, believed that women's failure to compete effectively
with men in certain areas of employment stems partly from the
imbalance in power between the sexes:

> GS: Could things be different? Could men do housework and
> women do 'tough' jobs?
> Steve (11 years, 2 months) I'm not sure about men being able to
> do women's jobs because men think that women were made to
> do housework.
> GS: Do *you* think women are made to do housework?
> Steve: Not really.
> GS: But why do they do it then?
> Steve: 'Cos men are more in charge and the woman often likes to
> please the man.

Similarly, Mandy said: 'Ladies don't [become firemen] because
men don't think they're capable', and Andrea, when asked why
men continue to go to work whilst women remain at home said:
'Maybe [men] don't want us to take over.' No 10 or 11 year old at
Workington mentioned the relative powerlessness of women and
only two pairs referred to the existence of social pressure (in the
form of stereotypes) when accounting for gender divisions
within the labour force. The provenance of these stereotypical
notions, however, was either unknown to the vast majority of
fourth-year juniors (from both schools) or was explained in
rather bizarre ways.

> GS: Where do we get our ideas from?
> Matthew: (10 years, 10 months) Our heads.
> GS: Before that?
> Matthew: People who made them up like God; people who
> organize things like the Labour Party, President or Prime
> Minister.

A few fourth years remarked on the influence of parental example in reinforcing commonly held conceptions of masculinity and
femininity, but only one child mentioned the role of television in
shaping these conceptions:

> Joanna: (11 years, 1 month) Girls think they have to be pretty all
> the time.
> GS: Where do girls get this idea from?

Joanna: From TV where women wear frilly dresses and have lots of make up.

A high proportion of Workington fourth-year juniors (in common with their Middleton peers) made comments implying that the origin of gender divisions in employment are innate or at least congenital. This was most noticeable in respect of references to 'physical attributes', but the single reference to personality differences suggested the same train of thought:

GS: Why do men seem to do some jobs and women do other jobs?
Ben: Women are meant to sit down and use their brains and men run around.
GS: We're made that way are we?
Ben: Yes, women are a bit more panicky.

Perceptions of unfair treatment

In order to elicit the children's views on unfair treatment in relation to gender, they were asked first to consider the best and worst aspects of life as a boy and as a girl. As far as Middleton infants are concerned, the best things about life as a boy are playing football, pursuing other non-domestic activities (such as 'riding my bike') and possessing distinctive toys and clothes. (This finding supports Livesley and Bromley's assertion that children below the age of 7 describe others predominantly in terms of their physical characteristics and routine actions.) The infants showed little awareness of unequal or preferential treatment. Middleton second years not only attached a high priority to playing football and other sports, but also saw physical attributes (notably greater strength) as a major asset. (Interestingly, it was at this age that Middleton children first displayed a marked tendency to explain occupational role in terms of physical strength.) There were also comments from the second years on the better employment prospects for boys. Not surprisingly, it was the oldest children at Middleton who were most cognizant of preferential treatment. They were aware not only of the extent to which boys benefit from stereotypes pertaining to 'women's work', but of boys generally having more freedom of action. Although the pattern of response at Workington was broadly similar, there were two main differences. First, a higher proportion of infants saw physical strength as one of 'the best things' about being a boy and, secondly, a much smaller proportion of Workington fourth years commented on the advantages of avoiding 'women's work'. Among both sets of fourth years, only one pair (from Workington) referred to preferential treatment in the context of school.

When considering the best things about being a girl, Middleton infants seemed to regard prevailing stereotypes as wholly advantageous. Most frequently they referred to conventional leisure pursuits, possessions and domestic activities such as 'cooking the dinner' and 'doing the housework'. The second years were conversant with a wider range of stereotypes especially those relating to unequal treatment (e.g. 'girls don't get told off as much') but were rather less enamoured of domestic chores. The 10 year olds' conception of preferential treatment embraced the possibility of discrimination against boys in school and against men in the labour market.

Among the more noticeable differences between Middleton and Workington infants was the lower rating given by the latter to domestic activities and the higher rating given to personality. (Girls were seen as more obedient, less 'grumpy' and as thinking 'that everybody loves them'.) A higher proportion of Workington infants also seemed to have difficulty in providing a sensible answer to the question.

There were a number of age-related differences in children's views on the worst things about being a boy. At both schools (but especially at Middleton) there was a greater awareness among the latter of the ways in which preferential treatment can manifest itself. The major difference between the 10 year olds and the two younger age groups in respect of preferential treatment was the 10 year olds' recognition that teachers, as well as parents and peers, can discriminate unfairly. A further difference between the two younger groups and the fourth years was the greater frequency among the latter of references to personality, the majority referring to boys' tendency to misbehave. (This perception may well have some basis in reality as recent research in infant and junior classrooms (cf. French and French 1986; Croll 1985) has shown that boys are more likely to be seen as presenting control problems.)

As far as the two schools are concerned, it would seem that children at Workington (especially the infants) were markedly more inclined to associate boys with aggression (and specifically with fighting) than was the case at Middleton. (This finding is further testimony to the importance that Workington infants apparently attach to physical strength as a social marker.)

In respect of the worst things about being a girl, only one Middleton infant referred to unfair or preferential treatment and that was in connection with domestic chores. The proportion of second- and fourth-year juniors who referred to such treatment was much higher. There was a similar pattern of response at Workington.

Turning now to consider the children's perception of men and women, the infants, in contrast to the remainder of the sample, showed almost no inclination to think in terms of preferential treatment. At Middleton, they considered the advantages of being a man chiefly from the standpoint of traditional leisure pursuits and various non-stereotyped activities such as going to work and 'going out to Chinese shops when they come home from work'. At Workington, the infants once again emphasized man's physical strength and also spoke favourably about his stereotyped roles such as those of builder and repairer. (As with their response to previous questions, it was the 8/9 year olds at Middleton, rather than the infants, who focused on man's physical qualities.)

There was a marked shift in the pattern of response between the infants and second-year juniors at Middleton in that the older children displayed more awareness of the advantages that men enjoy over women and the particular advantages they enjoy in the labour market. At Workington, the same developmental trend was apparent but seemed to occur later; that is, between the ages of 8 and 11. There were, in fact, only two infants (one from each school) who intimated that employment opportunities overall may be skewed in favour of men:

GS: What are the best things about being a man?
Sean: (7 years, 1 month) Men have got more money 'cos they get a job.
GS: Don't women get a job?
Sean: Sometimes, but men often get jobs more.
Andrew: (6 years, 11 months) [If you're a man] there's all sorts of different jobs you can do and women normally stay in the house. I'd rather be outside.

Some of the second-year juniors, when asked to explain gender inequality in the labour market, tended to blame the victim in the sense of attributing either physical or personality defects to women:

> *Ben*: [I'd rather be a man] 'cos men get more choice of what they want to do: like you don't often see a girl doing electronics. I wouldn't like to be a housewife. I'd like to fly an aeroplane.
> *GS*: What stops women flying planes?
> *Ben*: Women are weaker and more frightened of things. A man will often just turn round and look at something when a woman will scream.

A number of 8 and 9 year olds were still under the impression that certain jobs could only be done by men or by women:

> *GS*: What are the best things about being a man?
> *Tom*: (9 years, 7 months) I can be a doctor.
> *GS*: Can't you be a doctor if you're a woman?
> *Tom*: No.
> *Nicola*: (9 years, 1 month) You can be a lady doctor. I've seen them.
> *Tom*: Yes, but they're called nurses though.
> *Nicola*: When I was in hospital, a lady doctor visited me.
> *Tom*: That was a nurse.
> *Nicola*: No it wasn't 'cos she was in a costume.
> *Tom*: You don't really have to wear a costume if you're a nurse.

Conclusions and Policy Implications

Charting the development of children's understanding of unfair discrimination in respect of gender shows that 6 and 7 year olds start with very little awareness of the issue. In this study, for example, they failed to recognize that employment prospects are skewed in favour of men and showed no understanding of occupational stereotyping as a *social process* acting differentially on men and women. The top infants were either unable to offer a plausible explanation for gender divisions in employment or accepted them as the inevitable outcome of innate differences. Similarly, when they were asked to consider the advantages and disadvantages attaching to the male and female sex role, there were very few references to unfair (preferential) treatment. Indeed, a substantial number of these children saw the traditionally domestic role of girls and women as positive attributes.

While the second-year juniors displayed some awareness that gender divisions in the labour market are not inevitable, many were either unable to account for their existence or offered an idiosyncratic and unconvincing explanation. In common with the infants, they lacked any appreciation of the power of stereotypes to generate inequality, but they were aware of unfair discrimination against women in respect of both paid employment and domestic labour.

For the most part, the differences between the 8/9 year olds' and the 10/11 year olds' conception of gender was one of degree rather than of kind. The latter were generally more cognizant of the different manifestations of unfair discrimination and, not surprisingly, had a more sophisticated understanding of the effects of stereotyping.

A number of differences between Middleton and Workington children of the same age have been pointed out, but whether these differences reflect the social class composition of the two schools, or some other factor, is not known.

The chief policy implication of this study is self-evident. For now that we know something of young children's understanding of gender differentiation, we clearly ought to utilize this knowledge in planning anti-sexist initiatives in the primary school. Specifically, teachers are now in a position to counter some of the myths and half-truths alluded to in the introduction to this chapter. For example, we have noted that whilst many 6/7 year olds believe occupational stereotypes are in some sense inevitable, a number of 8 year olds have begun to question this assumption. The pedagogic implication of such a developmental progression would appear to be that *direct* teaching about occupational stereotypes may be optimally effective if it commences, for the generality of children, round about the age of 8. This recommendation should not, of course, be seen as contradicting Bruner's (1960: 33) well-known dictum that 'any subject can be taught to any child of any age in an honest way'. Children can certainly be taught some of the underlying principles of occupational stereotyping whilst at infant school. We are simply suggesting, in accordance with Bruner's (ibid.) notion of the spiral curriculum, that the actual situation facing men and women in contemporary society should be addressed directly, and for the first time, when children are approximately 8 years of age. (In the light of this recommendation, it is interesting to note that there were only two infants who commented on the advantages that men enjoy over women in the labour market.)

We have also drawn attention to the tendency of some fourth-year juniors to explain gender inequality in terms of primary socialization. The absence of such comments from our younger respondents suggests that the age of 10 to 11 is when the majority of children are most receptive to explicit teaching about the role of the family in reproducing this form of inequality. The data further indicate that the fourth year of the junior school may be the best time to begin plugging the gaps in children's knowledge of the origin of stereotypes. For it will be recalled that whilst children of this age frequently intimated an awareness of stereotypes, only one referred to the role of television in influencing popular conceptions of masculinity and femininity.

The purpose of our study was to provide a more rational basis for planning anti-sexist initiatives in the primary school. We are aware of the limited contribution we have made to realizing this objective and of the need for more research. In particular, we urge the need for research into young children's understanding of other forms of structural inequality, for without this knowledge primary schools are unlikely to play an effective role in promoting social justice.

CHAPTER 3

Classroom Practices and Organization

ANDREW WINDASS

A Primary School
Northumberland
1 June 1987

Dear Mrs Smith,
   I would like to take this opportunity of inviting you to come along to the school with Amanda at 2 pm . . . We would also like to invite you to the Barbecue on Saturday, 11 July – tickets from members of the PTA committee.
                              Yours sincerely

                              Signature
                              (Headteacher)

What about Mr Smith? He has not been invited to accompany his daughter on her pre-school visit and the annual school barbecue is to remain an unexplored delight. Is it assumed that the primary school is the domain of young children and their mothers? And what of Amanda's mother? Is it an implicit assumption of the headteacher that Mrs Smith is married, belongs to a nuclear family and probably does not work? Before we look at the world of the primary school into which Amanda is about to enter, what of the world that she has 'left behind'; what will she have learned as a consequence of four plus years of exposure to the values and attitudes which represent 'reality' in Britain in the 1980s?
   It is not unreasonable to say that British children grow up with sex-stereotyped names, clothing, toys, games, books and comics

pre-school)

(Whyte 1983a; France 1986). By the time they are of school age, gender stereotypes are firmly embedded. Once in schools these stereotypes are reinforced rather than challenged (Evans 1982; Tizard *et al*. 1988). Several studies (Walum 1977; Delamont 1980) argue that parents choose pretty names for girls which are polysyllabic, 'more melodic and softer'. Girls' names are fussy, pretty and pert rather than serious. By contrast boys' names are short, hard hitting and explosive. Duly labelled, we find that Amanda (loveable) and Diana (moon goddess) will be adorned in pretty pink dresses, ribbons and bikinis while Eric (ever powerful, ever ruler) and Gary (firm spear) will be wearing this year's blue 'romper' suit, football scarves and rugby shirts. Amanda and Diana will be offered a world of toys and games directing them towards passive, home-centred, non-scientific and non-technical roles. Many girls are given nurses outfits, make-up kits, miniature kitchens and Sindy dolls while Eric and Gary are at large saving or threatening the universe as He-man, Bat-man or Spider-man. The general picture is one of males having the creative and interesting roles while females are pre-occupied with keeping themselves and their surroundings clean and with establishing relationships. Anecdotal evidence suggests that female sales staff are more likely to sell the 'simple' toys while males sell the scientific, complex items – electric racing car circuits and microscopes. Advertisements and displays on the lids of games frequently reinforce the image that boys play with computers whilst girls master baking skills.   external

An introduction into the literary world can do little to raise Amanda's flagging self-esteem. Typically, comics for the small child carry the following messages – females keep things and people clean, females provide food and drink, females tidy up after males, females help people and do good turns, females are nurses, males are doctors. Boys revel in action on football pitches and other planets, revealing qualities of bravery and team spirit whilst the heroines from girls' comics are deeply embroiled with boyfriends, becoming a ballerina or curing acne (Delamont 1980). British children are growing up in a gender-segregated world, their homes and communities have deeply internalized stereotypes of masculinity and femininity. It is possible to cite evidence of parental protection of 'unusual' interests and aptitudes in their children but the tolerance changes when a child leaves home for a playgroup, day nursery or primary school.

The primary socialization outlined above is simplistic and

singularly unjust to many gender-conscious parents, publishers and manufacturers but of necessity, I feel, the primary school needs to be placed in a wider societal context. Only in such a context does it become apparent that gender differentiates at all levels, from cradle to pension-book, and is a vital issue with practical social, economic and political implications for all members of our society.

The differences in the educational experiences of boys and girls have been measured in several ways. Some studies have attempted to measure the divisive consequences of schooling for girls and boys (Sutherland 1981; DES 1987a). Other studies have attempted to provide a more detailed case-study of particular classrooms and schools, examining the social construction of reality through observation of teacher-pupil interaction (Hough 1985; Stanworth 1981). Such qualitative research highlights the importance of teacher labelling procedures and peer group expectations in providing conformity to existing sex roles.

The claims of this research are much more modest. This chapter is the product of a secondment, sponsored by the Northumberland TVEI unit, the brief of which was to produce a series of recommendations for, examples of and resources for positive gender practice in schools. Given my brief and acknowledging that the children in Northumberland schools are predominantly white, any findings are unable to take into consideration implications of race. An inevitable consequence of my secondment was my visiting a wide variety of schools, both primary and secondary, in an attempt to unearth positive gender practice in action. An inevitable and unintended consequence was discovering that some schools are further up the road towards gender equality than others! Christine Skelton has already identified the differences between anti-sexist and equal opportunities education in the introduction to this book. The focus of the work in Northumberland schools is clearly on equality of opportunity rather than anti-sexism.

What follows is a series of observations, recollections and generalizations from incidents, routines and policies which in isolation may appear trivial but whose cumulative effect lay the foundations for long-term disadvantage, both economic and social, in the positions of adult women.

At a superficial, but nevertheless significant, level my meanderings around schools revealed that gender remained a largely unquestioned organizational principle. The 'girls' and 'boys' carved into stone to specify separate entrances, still visible in older rural primary schools, might have fallen into disuse but only marginally more subtle devices of differentiation persist. Class lists, registers and record cards were usually separate. In some instances lavatories, changing rooms, cloakrooms and even playgrounds were sex-specific. Such organizational arrangements were so common as to be taken for granted and therefore invisible. Some teachers regarded such arrangements as 'natural' and 'convenient' and seemed genuinely surprised that I should ask about them. School rules, too, could be seen as reinforcing sex roles. I wonder what effect such rules have on children's perceptions of appropriate behaviour for boys and girls when boys are not allowed to use the cloakroom, girls cannot wear trousers in school, girls but not boys can stay inside when it rains? Many of the daily routines of some of the schools visited revolved around and underlined the pupils' gender. Conversation with pupils suggested that teachers requesting pupils to line up and enter or leave the room by sex was common. Gender was also used as a disciplinary or motivational technique. In one rural middle school I was addressing a year group of pupils who gleefully informed me that one particular teacher refused to allow members of the opposite sex to sit next to each other, in her words because, 'you just know what they will get up to'. In the same school the Christmas Carol Service was preceded by a series of 'rehearsals' in assemblies. Increased volume and enthusiasm were encouraged by pitting girls against boys to see which group had the most impressive singing voice. Many of the pupils' responses revealed how it was the norm for males to carry video equipment, PE apparatus and the like while it was the girls' expected duty to arrange flowers, act as hostesses for visitors and so forth.

The early introduction into role-models was compounded by the fact that principal teachers were typically male whilst first-year classes tended to be taught by females. In effect pupils experienced seeing men in positions of authority while women were their assistants. Gender role models were provided not only by the teachers but also by the ancillary staff. Secretaries, supervisors, kitchen staff and cleaning staff were all female. The senior caretakers and members of the ground staff tended to be male. Thus in terms of staffing, schools are reinforcing the

Equal opportunity proposal!

divisions and assumptions of the wider society (Gray 1987).

The teaching of reading is in general terms an important area of early education. Too often, however, it has the latent function of reinforcing gender differentiation (Stones 1983; Wade 1986). My study of reading schemes in the schools visited during my secondment revealed two very obvious biases at work – females are under-represented and the 'cult of the apron' continues in that females are presented stereotypically (see Nilsen 1975). Whilst I accept that it is probably impractical to throw out all the old sex-stereotyped books, it does seem valid to use such material to highlight the issue of sex-stereotypification with pupils, to emphasize that nowadays mothers go out to work, fathers bath babies, men can be nurses and women can be engineers. Such intervention strategies are not to be taken lightly. My well-intentioned but ill-considered attempt to introduce one particular primary school to the delights of 'Miss Brick the Builder' and 'Miss Fanshawe and the Great Dragon Adventure' were singularly unsuccessful. Rows and rows of courteous, attentive pupils sat glued to my dramatic portrayals of fiery dragons, hapless princes, assertive princesses and fearsome Miss Fanshawes only to dismiss my educational initiative as bizarre and unconvincing. Clearly a single 'Listen with Mother' (Father/Parent) session needs to be supported and reinforced by explanation, discussion and, indeed, repetition.

Beyond reading as an essential component of primary school curriculum, children were being introduced to mathematics, writing, creative play and construction play. There did not appear to be any overt evidence that boys and girls were perceived as having different abilities in these areas. In general terms teachers did not say that any gender-based differences existed. It would be tempting in a study of this sort to present a convenient list of clear findings. This would represent a gross over-simplification and would rightly be seen as offensive by infant teachers. However, several themes did become apparent to me as I videotaped a number of sessions in nursery classrooms. I acknowledge the limitations of this observational approach in that my presence might well have affected the behaviour of both staff and pupils. The fact that my 4-year-old son appeared frequently on the video pointing to his 'invisible' father behind the camera suggested that at least one young pupil was not oblivious to my presence. That said, by watching children at play, choosing activities for themselves, by watching what they choose and how they behave during these periods it is possible to gain an insight into their self-image, role models and interaction strategies.

It seemed that even by the beginning of the infant school, in mixed classes, children were beginning to select single-sex groupings. I can only speculate as to the long-term social and academic implications of such a choice. Equally apparent was that, even at this age, boys were beginning to 'own the classroom' in terms of access to toys, teacher attention and 'winning' disputes. The longer-term consequences are clear as girls learn not to expect to win, while the boys expect, and indeed achieve, victory. The early establishment of classroom power relationships might go some way to explaining the reduced participation of females in secondary schools. The perceived 'naturalness' of the boisterous, aggressive boy by many teachers suggests that the development of intervention strategies are unlikely.

One teacher, acutely aware of the implications of such differentiation, made the significant point that even to organize the classroom to guarantee equal use of toys which had previously been monopolized by the boys was not an all-embracing solution to equality. In keeping with the findings of Janet Hough (1983) she observed that, even though as a teacher she could ensure that both sexes used the toys equally, it was apparent that some toys were used in different ways by the different genders. The play-house could become an army tent, water taps do make impressive guns and the conventional pan was easily translated into an unconventional helmet.

Another pattern which became apparent from my observations and my ever-present video camera was that an understanding of interaction patterns is vital in attempting to understand gender differentiation. Although it is extremely difficult to generalize, and the pattern is far more complicated than I might be proposing, it seems reasonable to suggest that the extent and variety of interactions employed by male and female pupils varies significantly. Whilst in any class there were both boys and girls who stood out for a variety of reasons, it is accurate to claim that in the majority of cases it was the boys who dominated the lessons (Morgan and Dunn 1988). It was the boys who placed more demands upon the teacher in terms of seeking advice, demanding attention or volunteering assistance (Swann and

Graddol 1988). It was the boys who physically dominated the classroom in terms of noise and movement. It was the boys who most frequently were heard laughing, shouting and advising. It was the boys who most frequently engaged in either physical or verbal altercations with their peers. Conversely, to borrow Dale Spender's (1982) concept of 'invisibility', the most frequent 'invisible' child in any classroom was the female. It was the girls whose names teachers had most difficulty in recalling, it was the girls who were less likely to draw attention to themselves and it was the girls who demanded less, and therefore received less, of the teacher's time and attention. As has been argued by many writers, it is male pupils who are more likely to be asked questions by teachers, are more likely to be praised by teachers, are more likely to be criticized by teachers and are more likely to be punished by teachers (Wheldall and Merrett 1988). In response to teacher stimulus it should come as no surprise that male pupils were more likely to join in discussion, originate discussion or to offer comments in class.

Such findings suggest that proposed solutions to gender inequalities in primary schools cannot be reduced to mere 'checklists' to guarantee that gender is not used gratuitously as an organizational principle. It is too simplistic to assume equality will be the result of ensuring that toys, books and equipment appeal to all pupils, that registers and queues are not organized on the principle of gender and that girls and boys are not portrayed in stereotypical roles. Such an approach would do a singular injustice to what is a most complex issue. Gender differentiation in the primary school is embedded in a complex web of taken-for-granted procedures and assumptions which exist throughout our society. This being so, to offer a series of guidelines for good practice, or to recount exemplars of positive gender practice encountered during my secondment would not provide a blueprint for success. It is in the level of consciousness of the teacher, in the classroom management skills practised and in the general ethos of the school that solutions might rest. It is equally imperative that the work of the school is not undermined, consciously or unconsciously, by the home.

Gender is 'on the agenda' in many Northumberland primary schools. In some schools it is the committed few teachers who, unsupported by resources or management, chip away at the entrenched, often unquestioned assumptions of the institution and their colleagues. In other schools, initiatives and policy statements abound from above, working parties, in-service training and resources guarantee that issues of gender inequality are constantly at the forefront of teacher and indeed governor and parent consciousness.

The curriculum is an obvious area which gives scope for innovation and the promotion of equality. The Equal Opportunities Commission would applaud those schools which are promoting science-based studies at the primary level. The oft-quoted 'justification' that the lack of scientific studies in the primary school is due to the preponderance of women teachers in such schools is singularly inadequate. Resources are available to encourage teachers to think in terms of infant science or junior engineering (see Appendix 2). Such awareness is vital, for whereas the lack of scientific teaching is often counter-balanced for boys by their early play activities and the types of experiences they have had with parents, most girls do not receive these supplementary experiences. A logical extension of such an idea would be to develop the co-operation of parents. One school did not consider it too early to arrange a parents' evening to introduce parents, through a range of talks, Equal Opportunities Commission literature and displays, to the realities of education for girls and its consequences for employment potential and ambition. It was the same school which was attempting to promote science education through the medium of technology. Practices had been designed to encourage the development of spatial awareness and experience with mechanical toys and puzzles. In addition, it is worth adding that artistic crafts such as knitting, weaving, sewing and needlework are also effective ways of developing fine motor skills and co-ordination for both boys and girls.

To enable pupils to develop their talents fully it is essential to question over-simplified assumptions about why certain subjects and careers are considered appropriate only for boys or only for girls. In the case of specific subjects, attempts have been made to counter traditional assumptions and materials. To counteract the fact that much history material is the history of men, one school considered it appropriate to develop oral history. Children's grandmothers were invited to talk about their lives in World War II. Certain historical topics – witch-hunts, suffragettes – might change stereotypical images of women. One teacher used drama as a way of helping children explore sex-role stereotypes. Kathy Joyce's publication (see Appendix 2) was particularly useful in this context.

Several schools felt that integrated sport could be justified in the primary school. Such a logic is sound in that physical differences regarding size, weight and strength are unlikely, and integration was seen as a successful means of encouraging a pleasing balance between competition and co-operation. Perhaps involvement in prestige sports such as soccer would help girls to develop a status, self-confidence and independence which they later seem to lack. One teacher's observation that doing PE together improves their behaviour to each other in other lessons is significant. She also noted that they were even playing games in playtime together which they had learnt in physical education.

Any consideration of the curriculum inevitably involves an investigation into reading schemes, initial reading books, picture books, story books and textbooks. Whilst no school that I visited claimed to have conducted detailed research into books available in the classroom or library, one school was in the process of setting up a working party to review the present range of reading schemes and other children's books, using sex discrimination as one evaluation criterion. 'Genderwatch' (Myers 1987) and Whyte (1983a) (see references) provide neat checklists which can be used to make a quick analysis of books/worksheets to ascertain whether they are giving a biased picture of the real world. The checklist could be simply modified for use by pupils. I acknowledge the initiative taken by my son's school whereby any reading book chosen by him is recorded in a diary which is signed by parents who are given an opportunity to comment on the appropriateness or otherwise of the choice. Any process to promote or encourage parental awareness of gender issues is to be applauded. Indeed if parents raise the issue of gender inequality in schools through such interactive processes as completing diaries, parents' evenings and the like, then schools will be forced to examine their assumptions and strategies. I was proud of my son at the Christmas fête when he queried the logic of having separate 'Lucky-dip' bins for girls' and boys' gifts – a Parent-Teacher-Association consciousness-raising exercise perhaps.

Sexism in books is not restricted to reading schemes, picture books and story books. Many textbooks include discriminatory illustrations or examples (Northam 1982; Bailey 1988). Within the context of educational cutbacks and out-dated resources it is the responsibility of all teachers to select textbooks which present a balanced sex-role attitude and in which not all doctors, divers and drivers are male and not all nurses, secretaries and primary school teachers are female. Many organizations now exist to provide recommended readers (see Appendix 2). Where, of necessity, books are used which employ sexist or stereotypical words and images the teacher can use such material to point out to pupils the inappropriate messages carried. One teacher had taken this theme further in that her classroom wall supported an enormous collage which portrayed a media representation of females depicted through newspapers, advertisements, magazines etc. On the adjacent wall was a somewhat smaller collage attempting to portray the reality of females.

As considered earlier, the organization and day-to-day management of schools can do much to reinforce stereotyping. Logically therefore the reverse is applicable and organization and management can do much to counteract stereotyping. More schools are now becoming conscious that every effort should be made to present a non-discriminating environment. Many small but significant procedures are at work. I can hardly claim that my sorties into schools provided scope to evaluate the extent to which positive practices had been adopted with respect to the 'hidden curriculum'. However, conversations with teachers revealed that all or some of the above strategies are employed in Northumberland primary schools, or more particularly in specific classrooms. There still appears to be an absence of well-defined policy statements in a majority of the primary schools visited. However, in isolation, individual teachers are recognizing that there are alternative ways of calling a register to boys' names first then girls' names. Equally there is no obvious reason for insisting that boys and girls line up separately to move about the school, or that they should be segregated in classroom and assembly seating arrangements. Physical differences at primary school age cannot explain why boys usually carry the milk crates and PE equipment whilst the girls put out the paints and welcome the visitors. Raised teacher consciousness now allows girls to operate the school's audio-visual or other mechanical aids. There still remain, however, obvious areas of division. In terms of uniform girls are often required to wear restricting and impractical skirts while only boys are allowed to wear trousers.

School playgrounds are often informally segregated into areas for boys and areas for girls. Boys tend to monopolize the playground with football, the result being that girls have little alternative but to be onlookers. The exceptions to this pattern are those schools which promote mixed team games in PE lessons and which have a visible and aware staff presence at breaks or during lunchtime.

It is still apparent in too many classrooms and schools that one of the most important messages that pupils receive is that they are a boy or girl. Any teacher who maintains that it is because of traditional role expectations that girls do not achieve and then proceeds to underline the importance of gender is reinforcing inequality. Some schools have adopted strategies intended to counteract inequalities similar to those given by Gibbs in Chapter 8.

It is in the infant classroom and in the interaction patterns it contains that gender differentiation exists, often in hidden form. A self-fulfilling prophecy could be suggested if teachers expect girls to be more artistic than boys, if they expect boys and girls to behave differently, if they excuse behaviour in boys which would not be tolerated in girls. Teachers should avoid gender stereotyping when asking pupils for assistance, they should avoid assumptions that traditional family structures are the norm and that mothers and fathers have clearly defined areas of responsibility. The classroom should be a place where the pupil is encouraged to realize his or her full potential. This ideal situation cannot become reality, however, if teachers are more sarcastic to boys and more respectful to girls; if girls are expected to be more tidy in their uniform, in their ways and in their work, neater in handwriting and in their presentation of material.

My quest for positive gender practice in Northumberland schools highlighted the fact that any school faces two problems. The first is that much of the discrimination that goes on in schools is deeply hidden and not treated as problematic. As a generalization, teachers see girls as having different traits from boys and deem these characteristics 'natural', or the product of a wider society (see Skelton 1985). They do not question the necessity for their permanence or even their emergence in school life. The government can legislate against different curriculum and resource allocation but cannot make laws about teachers' attitudes any more than legislation can change racial prejudice.

The second problem is that schools do not exist in a vacuum. School is just one of the influences in a child's life; the family, peer group and the media need to be acknowledged as encouraging traditional sex stereotyping.

Any equal opportunities strategies, although going some way to ensuring that girls have equal access to the same education as boys, do not tackle inequalities of power which exist outside the classroom. Thus, whilst applauding the initiatives of individual teachers, such initiatives need to be set against the prevailing ideology of patriarchy and dominant interests. To disaggregate the classroom from the politics of educational policies and patriarchal dominance would be to ignore restraints on individual teachers. In addition to such external factors an array of internal conditions within an individual school need to be considered. Setting aside the personal capacities of individual teachers, such internal conditions might be seen to include the ideology of the headteacher, specific teacher union policy, school governors, the Parent-Teacher Association, the facilities of the school, and of course, the pupils themselves. All could have a significance with respect to sexist practice within the school.

In the context of Northumberland primary schools it appears that attempts are being made at an individual rather than an institutional level. What does appear to be needed is an awareness of the contribution that the school as a whole can make to promoting gender equality. This would lead to a questioning of the necessity and indeed the function of all the attitudes towards women that it transmits. Anti-discrimination legislation can go some way to obviating anomalies in education, but until administrators and teachers recognize the impact, or even the existence, of unequal conscious and unconscious policies and attitudes towards girls, it is likely that they will continue unchallenged much longer than clearly perceived areas of discrimination.

Primary Teachers

CHAPTER 4

And So The Wheel Turns . . . Gender and Initial Teacher Education

CHRISTINE SKELTON

On his final teaching practice, Alan took 'Space' as his theme for the work he was doing with a second-year junior class. The situation I witnessed on the first occasion I went into Alan's classroom to observe him teaching was one I had seen many times before. The children had been put into groups and were looking up information to complete worksheets on space travel, astronauts and satellite stations. Half the class appeared to be deeply engrossed in the work and, as I wandered around the room, I heard heated debates going on as to the merits of various rockets. However, other children were clearly totally uninterested and adopted the type of ploys familiar to all teachers. Repeated requests were made to Alan or myself to be allowed to 'go to the toilet', or 'sharpen my pencil', or children sat quietly fiddling with pencils whilst others chatted to their neighbours about what they would be doing after school. Not an unusual situation in any class perhaps, but what was striking was that, without exception, all the children who showed an interest in the work were boys whilst the girls demonstrated their boredom with the set tasks. After the lesson was over I talked to Alan about his observations of the session. Without any prompting on my part he said:

> I don't think it went very well . . . some of the kids really enjoyed the work . . . but . . . well, for instance Leanne and Jane kept fussing about whether they could go to the library to get more books and they unsettled their group and Joanne upset her group by arguing all the time about the crayons. I don't know why they

didn't just get on with it . . . when I was at school I used to think it
was great when we did anything about space.

What Alan had not considered in planning this work was that
what he had found motivating as a male primary school pupil
might not have the same impact on other children and particularly the girls. The upshot of our conversation was that Alan
decided to re-think his planning and the next time I visited his
school I saw books the children had compiled on women astronauts and women scientists.

The unfortunate fact remains that Alan was reaching the end
of his initial teacher education (ITE) course with apparently no
understanding of the role of gender within primary schooling.
The problem is that we know very little about how gender issues
are (or are not) tackled on ITE courses. What we do know is
that gender stereotyping is a feature of primary schooling
(Clarricoates 1980; Hough 1985) and we can assume that today's
student teachers are likely to have experienced discriminatory
attitudes and practices when they attended school. For example,
as pupils, students may have been exposed to the differing
attitudes teachers displayed towards them and their peers by
virtue of their sex; they may have 'learned' that boys are noisier,
more disruptive and better at technical subjects, whilst girls are
quieter, less adventurous and better at reading. It is not unreasonable then to find instances where student teachers repeat
many of the subtle discriminatory practices they were exposed to
as school children. Only since the Sex Discrimination Act (1975)
has equal educational opportunities as a mode of practice
become a factor which schools are expected to consider. Judging
by the handful of research articles which exist it seems that this
idea has only recently begun to be taken on board by ITE courses
(Whyte 1983b; Everley 1985; Hanson 1987). As with the discriminatory practices found to take place in nursery, primary
and secondary schools we need to find out what role gender
plays within ITE in order to develop strategies which can reduce,
if not remove, gender stereotyping. The intention then in this
chapter is, first of all, to identify the part gender plays within
primary initial teacher education by examining official guidelines
offered to ITE institutions. The second part of the chapter is a
case study of a Post Graduate Certificate in Education (PGCE)
primary course at All Saints College in which gender issues,

although not a feature of the official content structure, were an integral element of the 'hidden curriculum'.

The 'official word' on equality

From the early 1980s onwards and following the 1975 Sex Discrimination Act, agencies responsible for validating ITE courses in this country included specific reference to gender discrimination in their published guidelines. These guidelines focused on two areas where gender-discriminatory practices could arise: in the selection of students for the course and in the content of the initial teacher education programme. The Council for National Academic Awards (CNAA), who are responsible for validating all ITE courses offered by colleges of education and polytechnics, states:

> The Council is anxious that all institutions consider the implication of the legislation (Sex Discrimination Act) when devising courses, and endeavour not only to abide by the letter of the law, but also to implement the spirit of the Act. (1980: 69)

This document goes on to say:

> These considerations should be taken into account when devising a course and admitting students, and also in the subsequent conduct of a course. (1980: 69)

Similarly the Council for the Accreditation of Teacher Education (CATE) prepared a digest in 1985 of the criteria required from initial teacher education courses. The criteria concerning gender discrimination were originally laid down in the Department of Education and Science Circular 3/84 (Welsh Office Circular 21/84).

Regarding the selection of students for ITE, CATE recommend that:

> 1.3 The procedures should provide equal opportunities at all stages for all candidates, regardless of race or sex. (1985: 1)

In addition, within educational and professional studies:

> 5.8 Students should be prepared for the diversity of ability, behaviour, social background and ethnic and cultural origins encountered in ordinary schools; and in how to respond to that

diversity and guard against preconceptions based on race or sex. (1985: 3)

More recent official documents suggest, however, that there is a move *away* from considering gender issues on primary ITE courses. In a survey by Her Majesty's Inspectors (DES 1987c) there is no mention of gender or sexism in the sections relating to primary education. Similarly, The National Curriculum 5–16, with its emphasis on a core curriculum and testing, puts pressure on ITE institutions *not* to address equality issues within primary courses. The National Curriculum provides little flexibility for schools to build in areas of the curriculum which fall outside the core subjects and this has implications for the devising of primary ITE courses. In the consultative document (1987b) it was asserted that:

> Initial teacher training institutions should prepare students progressively for the national curriculum and the new assessment arrangements as these are designed and introduced. (p. 28)

The early 1980s witnessed the first attempts, albeit half-hearted, by CATE and CNAA to alert ITE institutions to the ways in which gender discrimination might operate. But even these small initiatives are being eroded as gender issues fail to obtain recognition in more recent documentation. If the future of gender inequalities as an area to be included in ITE programmes looks pretty gloomy, what influence has the recommendations of CATE and CNAA had on existing ITE courses? To attempt to answer this question and explore the various ways in which gender issues can affect the ITE experiences of student teachers we can consider the findings of a case study carried out at All Saints, a college of education in the north of England.

All Saints College

The research carried out with the PGCE primary course at All Saints demonstrated how gender issues can affect initial teacher education courses from recruitment through to the 'finished product'. There were twenty-one students on the course, only four of whom were males. Mrs Taylor, the course co-ordinator, said that the difference in ratio reflected that of the applications the college received. However, when we talked about interviewing prospective students, Mrs Taylor gave an indication of how deep-seated gender-stereotypical beliefs can affect a candidate's chances of selection. In this case female candidates were more likely to be offered a place on the course than males. Lee (1987) has remarked that many teacher educators hold the misguided view that male applicants for primary education courses should receive positive discrimination as they are in short supply! Mrs Taylor's attitude to this was:

> My husband said that we should take more men onto this course as more men are needed in primary schools. I argued that we weren't going to take in equal proportions for the sake of it but want the best people . . . those displaying the right personal characteristics such as commitment, caring, enthusiasm, sympathy . . .

The 'personal characteristics' she refers to are a factor stressed by the government in several of its documents relating to ITE, although the term 'personal qualities' is generally used (DES 1982; 1983; 1987c). For example:

> In our view there can be no justification for admitting to initial teacher training individuals who, academic competence apart, lack the qualities likely to enable them to become successful teachers, even if this leads to shortages in some areas. (DES 1983: 32–33)

At the time when I spoke to Mrs Taylor none of the official documents said precisely what these 'personal qualities' were that interviewers should be looking for. So it was very much a case of interviewers having to depend solely on their beliefs about what personal qualities primary teachers should have. In Mrs Taylor's case it would be wrong to suggest that in her view 'the best people' for primary teaching are females since no evidence was given to support such an idea. However, we do know that primary teaching is a predominantly female occupation and that it is commonly seen as a job which requires many of the same skills as those found in child rearing (Deem 1978). When Mrs Taylor referred to such characteristics as 'caring' and 'sympathy', qualities more often associated with females than males, she may have unconsciously brought into play during interviews deep-seated notions of gender together with her expectations of what a primary teacher 'is'. This is what Jenkins (1986) refers to as 'suitability' and 'acceptability' criteria used by interviewers. A person's suitability for a particular post can be demonstrated by such areas as academic qualifications or previous experience of the job. But the non-specific criterion of acceptability depends for its interpretation on the taken-for-granted knowledge, attitudes and prejudices of interviewers. As primary teaching is mainly a female career it is not unreasonable to suggest that interviewers may unconsciously favour female candidates on the basis of their taken-for-granted knowledge about *who* enters primary teaching.

Having said that, although with regard to acceptability criteria female candidates for the course at All Saints may have stood a better chance than males at being offered a place, this did not apply to all females. The 'mature' students on the course were those who were aged 25 and above; the oldest student on the course was in fact 28. Mrs Taylor said that only applicants under the age of 30 were interviewed as 'they are more likely to obtain teaching posts'; more likely presumably than students in their late 30s and 40s. Spencer and Podmore (1987) have pointed out that many women, unlike men, have broken or bimodal career patterns to allow for bearing and rearing children. They go on to say that the late 20s and early 30s are often a crucial period of career life and it is precisely those years in which many women find family commitments are at their most demanding. Consequently, those adults, the majority of whom are likely to be women, that opt for teaching as a career in their 30s would be discriminated against by All Saints. One would like to think that the adopting of unofficial age barriers was a strategy unique to All Saints but in my own experience as a teacher-educator I have come into contact with other ITE institutions, including those with 'Equal Opportunity' policies, who administer similar age barriers – a common age limit is set at 35.

Clearly the recommendations of CATE and CNAA regarding the recruitment of students to ITE courses would seem to be inadequate. Both CATE and CNAA needed to implement and monitor their recommendations. A useful start might have been if ITE institutions had been given some guidance as to the ways in which sex discrimination could take place in recruitment, from application form to interview. Of course it may be that this was not done simply because neither CATE nor CNAA had thought through the issues surrounding recruitment themselves.

The students who were accepted by All Saints undertook a

programme format common to many PGCE courses. The first term was divided into two parts – an introduction to teaching which was campus based followed by a block teaching practice; the second term was mainly campus based in order to concentrate on Professional Studies; the final term was given to a block teaching practice. All Saints did not include gender as a topic within the Professional Studies element of the course nor was it raised as an issue by any of the curriculum area tutors. Yet gender did form a part of the hidden curriculum of the course. The emphasis placed at All Saints on child-centred approaches, the schooling experiences and adaptive strategies of the students, and the teaching methods used on the course conspired to reproduce the gender-stereotypical attitudes and practices found in many primary schools (Clarricoates 1978; Delamont 1980; Hough 1985). Each one of these will be considered to demonstrate how, by treating gender as a non-issue in primary education, discrimination was actively perpetuated.

Alexander (1984) following King (1978) has pointed out that the ideology of child-centredness comprises four elements, one of which is individualism: that is, where teachers need to respond to children as unique individuals. It was the emphasis given to individualism which appeared to be the major contributory factor to the students' idea of gender-stereotypical practices as an issue inapplicable to the education of primary school children. Constantly students were told that work prepared for school practice had to be based around the individual needs of each child in the class. There is no reason to suppose that by allowing children to develop at an individual pace gender discrimination will be prevented. Children are socialized into gender categories by factors other than just the school, namely their families, peer group and the media. In one school we visited the gender implications for catering for the individual needs of each child were clearly demonstrated.

The theme the class of third-year juniors were working on was Houses. A variety of tasks had been set out by the teacher for the children to choose from. After the introduction to the lesson the teacher told the children they could select the task they would like to work on. Amongst the activities going on the student teachers saw a group of boys involved in constructing an electrical circuit for a doll's house and a group of girls designing patterns for curtain materials. Was this simply a matter of

children recognizing their own individual needs that resulted in
an all-male group pursuing a traditionally male-associated task
and girls a traditionally female one? When I spoke to the girls,
two of them said they had chosen to work on the painting
activity but of the other three, one had wanted to experiment
with the electrical circuit, one would have liked to help build a
bird table and the third had initially opted for the pottery wheel
to make household pots. When I asked why they had not
responded to their own 'needs' they said that the boys had got to
the electrical circuit and the pottery wheel first and the girl who
had wanted to help build a bird table had been put off because
she would have had to work with a group of boys. Thus, providing opportunities for children to develop according to
their 'individual needs' does not take into account the gender
power relationships within the classroom. It was not uncommon
for students to visit schools where boys could be seen to be doing
'boyish' things such as commandeering practical equipment, and
fist-fighting when the teacher's back was turned, whilst, for the
most part, girls were pushed to the periphery of the classroom
in a literal and metaphorical sense. As the implications for
gender of the scenes we witnessed in the classroom were never
raised by tutors, it was not surprising that the students saw
catering for individual needs of children as a way of preventing
stereotyping:

> Gill: It's possible to get rid of stereotyping by unstructured play
> . . . get the girls to use the Meccano. For all children to get
> every experience they can want.

One of the other elements of child-centred education is that of
Play as Learning (Alexander 1984) and this too was a point
frequently referred to by tutors. The students would be *told* they
should use teaching methods which would encourage children to
learn through their own experiences as this was when *real*
learning took place yet tutors adopted teaching approaches
which were totally incompatible with the espoused theory. HMI
commented in a recent report (DES 1987c) that probationary
teachers arrive in schools still needing a great deal of help and
guidance. To resolve this they suggest that ITE institutions pay
greater attention to developing student teachers' critical and
reflective abilities:

Students should become accustomed to question, to debate, to

analyse, to argue from evidence, and to examine their
habitual assumptions. (p. 30)

The student teachers at All Saints were not given the time to
think through the ideas they were being introduced to and the
framework of individual sessions did not encourage questioning
or debate. The students were timetabled from 9 am to 5 pm five
days a week. Wednesday afternoons were, in theory, allocated
to 'personal study' but in effect were often used for visits to field
centres, special schools and industry. This meant that evenings
and weekends were the only times when assignments could be
written and work prepared for school practice so no time
remained for reflection. Similarly the tutors adopted teaching
methods within curriculum areas which did not promote opportunities for debate and analysis. A common scenario was for a
tutor to talk whilst the students took notes and then students
would carry out a practical activity which they could repeat
with children. In effect, the students took on the role of primary
school children whilst the tutor acted the role of primary teacher.
The irony of the situation was not always lost on them as it was
not unusual to see students raise their hands to answer a question, calling out 'Please Sir' to gain the tutor's attention or
ask if they could be 'scissor monitor' (maths) or 'brush monitor'
(art and craft). This very highly structured approach effectively
discouraged any opportunities for such cross-curricular issues
as race and gender to emerge which meant that not only were
students not being introduced to the discriminatory practices
which take place in the primary school but they were also not
provided with a platform upon which they could 'examine their
own habitual assumptions' regarding both race and gender.

To add to this situation certain 'tips' about the behaviour and
abilities of primary age girls and boys were occasionally offered
by teachers involved with the PGCE course as well as tutors.
Time and again I heard teachers pointing out a boy or a group of
boys that students would need to 'keep an eye on'. On one of
several occasions the PE tutor actively encouraged discriminatory practices. The students had been doing a series of very
slow, controlled body movements which the tutor followed up
by saying:

> You would need to use more vigorous activities for the kind of
> boy who gets no enjoyment from artistic movements.

At another time, a teacher who visited the college spoke to the students about the environmental studies work which took place at the school where he was deputy head. The talk was illustrated by a series of slides. One particular sequence of slides showed mammal traps being emptied, an activity carried out by boys. Immediately following on from this sequence was a slide of a girl standing in a field holding a clipboard:

> *Teacher*: This is Susan, who was ever so keen to get her photograph taken and said could she pretend she was recording. It was because she'd got a new skirt or something.

Throughout the slide showing the teacher would provide explanatory comments about the tasks shown on each slide but if a girl or group of girls appeared on a slide they were glided over with a basic statement such as 'This is Katy . . . she's in year one'. The impression was given that environmental projects require a high degree of involvement from boys whilst the girls stand around or pick flowers.

The students were also told certain 'facts' about girls and boys; that is, boys experience greater problems in learning to read, they are disruptive in the classroom and they are better at maths than girls (see Skelton 1987). However, as Jacklin's (1983) work has shown, physiology aside, there are few, if any, biological differences between girls and boys:

> In general intelligence, attention span, cognitive abilities and task orientation boys and girls are alike when they enter school. These are all areas relevant to school behaviour that do not differentiate the sexes. (pp 16–17)

The 'facts' that students were told about the abilities and behaviour of girls and boys are social facts rather than natural facts and, as such, some change in these circumstances is possible. The danger is that as student teachers were 'taught' these 'facts' as a part of their professional socialization it is possible that these messages might have been internalized and could affect their expectations of boys' behaviour and reading capabilities. What is of even greater concern is that the 'fact' that boys are better at maths in the primary school is inaccurate. We know that by the time girls reach examination stage at secondary school they are not succeeding in maths at the same rate as boys. This is not the situation in primary schools for there is a welter of research

(Assessment of Performance Unit 1982; Walden and Walkerdine 1985) which confirms that during the early years of schooling girls do better on average in most standardized tests of attainment. However, if student teachers are given the impression that boys are better at maths there is a possibility their professionally informed expectations may help to create a self-fulfilling prophecy.

The argument put forward so far has been one which has shown how the content and structure of All Saints primary PGCE course perpetuated and, to an extent, exacerbated, gender-stereotypical ideas and practices. At the same time, this argument provides only a one-sided perspective, suggesting that the student teachers were passive recipients in their professional socialization. This was certainly not the case; the majority of students held views concerning equality between the sexes. They were very quick to challenge sexist comments and behaviour but only in relation to stereotyped ideas which affected them as adults (see Skelton 1987). In their role as student teachers, some chose to overlook sexist practices whilst others were unaware of the gender stereotyping they were being exposed to.

Recent work by Andrew Pollard (1985, 1987) and Alastair Horbury (forthcoming) has shown how children utilize 'adaptive strategies' as primary pupils. Their argument is that children, as pupils, learn the rules and regulations of the classroom and set up a process of negotiation with the teachers whereby the needs of both are, to some extent, met. This model can also be applied to the students and tutors at All Saints. The main concern of the tutors was to ensure that the students were provided with enough 'ideas' to cope with teaching practice. These ideas catered for what Denscombe (1982) has identified as the major concerns of student teachers – that is, the course provided 'tips' on *what* to teach and *how* to control twenty-five plus children. The needs then of both tutors and students were, as far as possible, catered for. The students were provided with ideas for curriculum content and control and the tutors were fulfilling their part by passing on teaching 'knowledge'. Whilst this strategy, appeared to satisfy many of the students, one or two were unhappy about operating in a situation which did not allow for wider discussion. Two of the female students Alison and Cheryl, were open about their political beliefs. They had been actively involved with women's groups during their undergraduate days and had some understanding of the gender discrimination which takes place in schools. However, they both decided to keep their attitudes towards sexism in schools 'under their hat' because they felt their career prospects would be marred. Alison had quickly come to realize that her obvious political views were not seen as an asset by the course tutors. This had not been made known to her overtly, but any political statements she made were received with what she called a 'patronizing smile'. She was often asked to have tea with the co-odinator because, as she said, the tutors felt she was not fitting in comfortably with the rest of the group. After contesting much of the course content during the first term Alison decided that she would either have to leave the course or learn not to raise questions concerning the implications gender and class had on the educational theories being introduced. In a similar way Cheryl realized as soon as she had started the course that if she wanted to get a good reference for a teaching post she would have to curtail any comments that might be construed as 'political'. In order for Alison and Cheryl not only to 'survive' the course but to obtain references which would indicate their ability to 'fit in' with others, they felt it necessary to conceal their political beliefs – in this case to refrain from mentioning gender. For the majority of students, however, gender issues within primary schooling was an unrecognized concept.

Given the underlying ethos of the course and the teaching methods adopted it was not surprising to find students repeating discriminatory practices in the classroom. Whilst they avoided any obvious forms of discrimination, such as lining the children up in boys and girls, more subtle practices were clearly evident. In the same way that Peter at the beginning of this chapter was seen reverting to his own gender-stereotyped knowledge of what he had found interesting at primary school, so did many of the students at All Saints. The interesting feature here was that several of the female students prepared work on the basis of what the boys might find interesting and, in the main, encouraged boys to take a more active role than the girls. On one occasion two female students undertook an environmental studies project with a group of children. The boys were given clipboards and asked to record information on the measurements of the hedge, provided with jars to collect insects and asked to set up a mammal trap. The girls were told to pick flowers! At another time a female student planned an afternoon's work centred around the making of radio programmes. The boys took on the roles of newscaster, weatherman, interviewer, quizmaster and contestants as well as operating the radio cassette. This left the girls making up 'jingles' to play in between the programmes and designing posters and badges to advertise the radio station.

Equally evident were the preconceptions they demonstrated of the abilities and behaviour of girls and boys. Both of the following observations took place two-thirds of the way through the ITE programme. A tutor was discussing with a group of students some examples of poetry which children had written in their own handwriting but without putting their names on:

Jack: This is neat handwriting . . . was it a girl who wrote this?
Tutor: No, a boy.
Jack: A boy!
Lucy: No, I wouldn't have said it was a boy's handwriting either.

A few days later we visited a school and sat in on a music lesson. After the lesson had finished some of the students talked to the class teacher:

Jack: The children all seem to enjoy singing.
Teacher: Yes they do. They're all keen to sing solo at any concerts we have . . . even the boys.
Jack: There was certainly lots of volume coming from the back.
Colin: (laughing) Yes . . . the back row of boys.

On neither occasion did the tutor or teacher attempt to encourage the students to discuss their stereotypical reactions, and other students in the group also failed to comment on their colleagues' stereotyped assumptions. What is more, this lack of response could be seen as a confirmation of their observations. Frequently, tutors and teachers would discuss with students points of organization, teaching methods and curriculum content. In this way students were encouraged to reassess their ideas in the light of others' professional opinions and so, to some extent, they relied on these discussions with experienced teachers to clarify some of their own notions about primary teaching. When teachers and tutors fail to get them to question their assumptions that 'boys make more noise' and 'girls are neat handwriters' they are, in effect, confirming students' preconceptions. It is fair to say that, if students are allowed to persist with their taken-for-granted notions of boys' and girls' abilities and behaviours, then, as teachers, they are likely to perpetuate gender stereotyping.

Conclusion - Conclusion .

over that

The Sex Discrimination Act (1975) is now (more) than a decade old and equal educational opportunities as actual classroom practice is an aspect of schooling teachers are encouraged to consider by the EOC (Equal Opportunities Commission) and many LEAs. Initial teacher education provides an obvious opportunity for student teachers both to confront their own gender-stereotypical assumptions and to be introduced to where and how gender discrimination takes place in schools. At the moment there is no quantitative information available as to the number of ITE institutions which have incorporated gender into the official course content. From the limited information which does exist it appears that, where gender issues are given an official platform, a variety of approaches are used: that is, in 'one-off' lecture slots, consigned to optional courses or permeated throughout the programme. This latter approach is, as Hanson (1987) points out, by far the most effective method provided that the implementation of equal opportunity initiatives is monitored and not simply left to the whims or knowledge of individual tutors. The study of the PGCE primary course at All Saints College demonstrates that where gender issues are not addressed they still permeate the programme but reinforce rather than reduce gender-stereotyped ideas. A cyclical process developed whereby the gender-discriminatory practices students experienced as primary school children were reinforced by the ITE course and subsequently repeated on school practice. The course offered by All Saints adopted what Britzman (1986) has identified as a typical approach to initial teacher education:

> Indeed, the dominant model of teacher education is organized on an implicit theory of immediate integration: the university provides the theories, methods and skills; schools provide the classroom, curriculum and students; and the student teacher provides the individual effort; all of which conspire to produce the finished product of professional teacher. (p. 442)

As she says, this model ignores the social and political context of teacher education whilst emphasizing the individual's efforts. Many writers have argued that by stressing the responsibility of the individual teacher within the schooling process, so-called 'political' issues, such as race, gender and class, are not seen as having a place in the primary classroom (Lee 1987; Carrington and Troyna 1988). The PGCE primary course at All Saints operated on this model and hence allowed students to negotiate and side-step so-called 'controversial issues' by adopting teaching techniques which effectively precluded students confronting their habitual attitudes and assumptions.

It is perhaps not surprising that recent studies have shown that the educational experiences of boys and girls have changed very little in the years which have elapsed since the Sex Discrimination Act when many ITE courses adopt the model put forward by Britzman (1976). Rather than promoting wider thinking in student teachers, such courses discourage questioning and analysing the nature of primary schooling. Lee's (1987) study of infant teachers discovered that one of the effects of initial teacher education is *not* to promote a critical, political or social consciousness in teachers. The effects of the PGCE programme at All Saints on students' attitudes towards gender issues in the primary school are summarized in the views of Rachel. Her comments provide a disheartening picture for those teachers working in individual schools promoting gender awareness amongst colleagues who may anticipate that at least new recruits will have been introduced to gender inequalities during their ITE:

> *Rachel*: I think it's a result of the educational system having different expectations of boys and girls. I think we should just see them as individuals . . . boys and girls are different and it's daft to try and change it. They all have gifts which have to be developed and when they excel they should be encouraged. . . . I don't *really* see anything wrong in, say . . . girls being allowed to do woodwork.

CHAPTER 5

Teacher Attitudes: Complacency and Conflict

BARBARA THOMPSON

The scene is a primary school staffroom. The Equal Opportunities representative is pinning up a notice from the Equal Opportunity Support Group, inviting all interested parties to an evening meeting at the Educational Development Centre the following week. The issue to be discussed is, 'Do you provide "Equal Opportunities" in your classroom?' The following comments are made by various members of staff:

> I don't see what all the fuss is about, we treat them all the same anyway.

and,

> Oh not that left-wing rubbish again! What's it got to do with teaching?

One or two people shift uncomfortably in their chairs and say nothing. No-one says that they would like to attend the meeting, despite the attempts of the Equal Opportunities representative to explain that gender is an important issue and one which directly affects primary education.

The actual scene is fictitious but in my experience both as a primary school teacher and as a researcher into primary initial teacher education, these reactions are by no means uncommon. In the main, the attitudes of many primary practitioners appear to fall into these two categories: that is, some teachers demonstrate complacency whilst others are hostile to the gender question. Furthermore, because these two attitudes are so widespread, those teachers who might be interested in finding out about gender inequalities may be dissuaded from doing so, for fear that they might invite disdain or humour from colleagues.

Attitudes towards gender differentiation within education have historical, structural and ideological roots which are complex, deep seated and resistant to change. Amongst others, Brah and Deem (1986) have argued that to tackle attitudes and overt behaviour alone is not enough. This may be the case, but attitudes do remain of fundamental importance (see Byrne 1978). The attitudes and beliefs that teachers hold of 'boys' and 'girls' are transmitted through the 'hidden curriculum' to their pupils. Such 'facts' as boys are better at mathematics than girls and such messages as 'boys carry the heavy PE equipment' are perpetuated from one generation of primary school teachers to another (see Skelton 1985).

From my own experience it has become apparent that of all the sectors of education it is the primary field which is the most resistant to addressing the 'gender question'. The majority of research concerned with pupils of school age has been centred upon the secondary age band with its more visible areas of gender discrimination such as subject choice and examination results (Deem 1978; Scott 1980; Kelly 1982; Whyld 1983; Whyte 1986). Studies of sex role stereotyping in the primary field are far fewer in number. Those that do exist indicate that gender discrimination exists at a more covert level, infiltrating all areas of school life (Lobban 1978; Clarricoates 1978; Delamont 1980; French and French 1984). As Everley (1983) has stated, the primary years are crucial to the formation of attitudes towards the question of gender and it is, therefore, disturbing to find that many primary teachers are complacent or hostile to gender inequalities in the classroom.

Many teachers undertake their initial education courses straight from their own school classrooms. Traditional attitudes towards gender that have been formed from home, peer groups, media and school experience remain, in many cases, unchallenged and intact, Hanson and Herrington (1976) state:

> The preparation of teachers does not begin in college but in infant schools. Students entering college already know what teaching is. (p. 12)

If this is the case and they know what teaching 'is', it might be assumed that during their own school experiences they may also have learned certain stereotypical ideas about the abilities and behaviour of girls and boys. If they are not given the opportunity either in initial teacher education or when they become classroom teachers to actively challenge the attitudes and beliefs that they hold towards gender, then it is likely that stereotypical and/or discriminatory practices will continue.

It is true that within many LEAs teachers are given the opportunity to examine their attitudes to sex role stereotyping. Some LEAs are now 'Equal Opportunities' authorities, some have equal opportunities advisory teachers and many schools have 'Equal Opportunities' representatives. The fact remains that a large proportion of those involved in the primary field do not seem to think that gender is an issue which affects them.

In 1983 an LEA with which I was involved declared itself an Equal Opportunities Authority. This information was received by many primary teachers in the authority with much puzzlement, a certain amount of derision and a concern that they might have to consider 'left wing rubbish' which was in no way relevant to the job they were supposed to be doing. Those who did have an interest in gender issues eagerly awaited the arrival of new unsegregated registers and an official edict that such stereotypical practices as lining boys and girls up separately were to be discontinued. Nothing happened. In 1984 this situation appeared to alter as more positive moves were made. A letter was circulated to schools inviting interested parties to a meeting, after school, at the teachers centre to discuss the issue of gender and 'good classroom practice'. This letter was circulated not by the LEA but by the Equal Opportunities Support Group which had come together on a voluntary basis in the spring term of that year. Feeling that something was finally happening, I arrived at the meeting with a colleague from another primary school. We found that, apart from two women who were members of the Support Group, we were the only representatives from primary schools. The evening was devoted to discussion of the problems in secondary schools, and we failed to create an opening for the problems experienced in the primary sector. Secondary school staff did not appear to think that the issue of gender differentiation was as relevant to the younger age band. Their argument was that gender discrimination *really* affected girls' education when it came to subject choice in the secondary school. The failure of my colleague and me to influence this attitude made me realize that it is almost impossible for isolated individuals, particularly those in relatively powerless positions, to create change. The problems of isolation were reinforced when, sometime later, 'Equal Opportunities' representatives were appointed in schools. With very few exceptions, primary representatives told the same tale of antipathy or antagonism. Attempts to 'raise the consciousness' of colleagues about such issues as whether segregation along the lines of gender was necessary or desirable or whether the images of males and females presented in reading schemes reinforced stereotyping were greeted in various ways. Teacher attitudes ranged from tolerant amusement or lack of interest to real antagonism. In most cases 'Equal Opportunities' representatives were the only members of staff who cared about gender issues and in many cases these isolated individuals were becoming distressed and discouraged. The problems encountered by those trying to conduct a solo campaign have been referred to by Ord and Quigley (1985). They state:

> Without the active encouragement of other people, the familiar syndrome of failure, resentment, giving up, is only too possible. It is frightening how quickly we run into hostility or dismissive amusement even when quite small changes are suggested and facing such reactions alone can be a daunting prospect . . . (p. 100)

The majority of primary teachers within the authority did not seem to regard gender as a matter that was relevant to them. Their complacency that 'everything was all right as it was' or their outright antagonism to the issue meant that attempts to create change were met with a great deal of resistance.

Why should this be the case? It is the intention of this chapter to examine some of the reasons underpinning primary teachers' resistance to 'the gender question' and also to discuss measures that may help pave the way to real and effective change.

In order to try and obtain some understanding of why so many primary teachers appear to hold either complacent or hostile views about gender and primary age children, I decided a useful starting point would be to 'trace back' teachers' careers to their initial training, my reasoning being that the ways in which sex role stereotyping and discrimination is tackled by initial teacher education is of critical importance if there is to be any possibility of reducing discriminatory practices in the classroom. My findings were that, for the majority of those involved in a primary BEd programme, the ideology of primary education and promoting gender equality were mismatched. That is, for the most part gender was not seen as something that was either relevant or even 'suitable' for consideration by prospective primary teachers (see Thompson 1986). As a result, only cursory treatment was given to any recommendation that sex discrimination be taken seriously (CNAA 1980; CATE 1985). Gender issues were marginalized, on the outskirts of programmes, a matter for concerned individuals rather than a central concern. Just as I had found in school, the most prevalent attitudes amongst staff and students were those of complacency or hostility.

Complacency and ITE

The attitude of many primary teachers that I have met towards the question of gender is that it is unnecessary to make a fuss about an issue that is really 'not a problem'. Primary school teachers feel they treat all children the same, as individuals, so how can they be guilty of discriminatory practices? (Everley 1983; Hough 1985.) The same attitude was prominent amongst many students and staff on the initial primary BEd course. As many of them did not perceive any problem, they saw no reason to pursue the subject further. There was an opportunity for students to take a course on gender, albeit as a second option choice, which was only available in the first year. However, not even the two students who did show concern with gender had elected to take this option. In their case, however, it was for reasons pertaining to what they said were seen as suitable courses of study for prospective teachers, such as how to teach language skills to children by individual methods. Most students appeared happy in the knowledge that they themselves disagreed with traditional sex role stereotyping and would not be 'sexist' in their own teaching, so what was the fuss about?

It can be argued that this attitude shows a lack of any real awareness of the structured nature of gender discrimination within society in general, and within education in particular (Delamont 1983). Furthermore, as a result of this lack of awareness, in terms of classroom practice, it was believed by many that 'individualistic', child-centred approaches to teaching would lead to 'equality for all' (see Chapter 4).

Commitment to, and a deep understanding of, children as unique individuals is one of the main bases of primary teachers' professional claims (Alexander 1984: 21) The following comment epitomizes many of the students' attitudes:

> *Ernest*: I suppose a lot of schools still do have boys and girls lines, but I wouldn't. They should be treated as individuals.

The benefits of the child-centred approach were constantly reiterated by the students. Furthermore, their belief that sexism in the classroom was easily overcome led to irritation when the gender question was introduced by individual tutors.

> *Ursula*: Because it's made such a thing of . . . you tend to over-compensate for something that should be natural. A child should be taken on its own merits.

In fact, 'being made such a thing of' came down to the comments of one individual tutor in one particular seminar.

As in school, there were isolated individuals amongst both students and staff who had a real concern with gender. The individual members of staff raised the issue where they could, for example in discussions of sexism in children's books, but the priorities of the course were that primary BEd students should be involved with more 'relevant' issues. As one female student put it:

> When you're a BEd you're sort of pushed into the courses you should be doing. It would be seen to be frivolous, or a waste of time to do something like 'Women in Society'.

The majority of tutors also believed that child-centred approaches were a panacea for all ills:

> *Miss Wordsworth*: If you treat children as individuals all will be equal.

Other tutors did not see gender as relevant to their subject area:

> *Mr Jennings (Science)*: I don't think gender affects science. In a science experiment I don't recognize the colour of skin or any particular sex.

This attitude remained unchanged despite the recent studies and reports which highlighted current concern with girls and science (Kelly 1982; Whyte *et al.* 1985).

Complacent attitudes towards gender can be explained in two
ways: firstly, by lack of awareness and secondly, by the belief in
the effectiveness of individual approaches to the teaching of children. No one was aware that child-centred education has been
regarded by some commentators as militating against equal
opportunities or anti-sexist classroom practices being taken on
board (see Introduction). Many teachers, tutors and students
seemed to rest easy in the belief that gender is really not a problem
for the primary sector.

Hostility and ITE

As I had found in schools, antagonism to gender issues existed
amongst both students and staff and this hostility presented itself
in a number of ways. The discussion of sexism in children's books
mentioned earlier had been regarded by some students as 'offensive'. Two male students had walked out of the lecture. When
tackled by one of the female students the comment was made that
it was a complete waste of time bothering with 'rubbish like that'.
In other cases staff were hostile to those colleagues who had a
concern with gender. One feminist tutor commented scathingly:

> In this college *we* don't have any patience or tolerance. For exam-
> ple, a new member of staff wished to be known as 'Ms' and the
> comment was made immediately by three senior colleagues, '. . .
> we can't use that awkward term . . .' There is a sexist attitude on
> behalf of both men and women in the college which is very diffi-
> cult for students to resist.

However, it appeared that the students were actively affected by
such attitudes. One had been refused permission by a member of
the college staff to undertake a special study on gender, as the tutor
did not approve of the content. A second incident indicated that
resistance to gender came from a wider field than the college itself.
Another student disclosed that a study on gender had been refused
by her teaching practice school. Her tutor had commented:

> It's very difficult in a public sector like education, which at its
> roots is very resistant to change; very conservative . . . schools
> are very sensitive about subjects like gender . . .

Apart from my own personal experience of how sensitive or
antagonistic primary schools can be to the gender issue, studies

have shown that such reactions have by no means been uncommon. Delamont (1980) gives the example of a controversy which arose in Devon over a draft report on sex role stereotyping in primary schools. The education committee had rejected the report and had stated:

> If parents wish to bring up boys as boys and girls as girls, this would seem highly desirable and fundamental to family life. If boys are turned into fairies, and girls into butch young maids, it should be for parents to decide, and not the education authority or schools. (p. 11)

In order to attempt to offer an explanation for hostility it is necessary to look more closely at the nature of primary education. Numerous researchers suggest that both the nature of education and the existence of traditional sex role stereotyping within it has changed very little over the years (Young 1971; Sharp and Green 1975; Dale *et al*. 1981; Walker 1983; Alexander 1984). These commentators suggest that education is a patriarchal institution dedicated to maintaining and reinforcing gender-discriminatory practices which uphold the status quo. To quote just one source, Walker (1983) states:

> . . . schools operate so as to reproduce and sustain gender differentiated ideologies . . . (p. 1)

With particular reference to primary schools and teachers, Lee (1987) comments that:

> The sociopolitical views of . . . teachers [are] remarkable for their insignificance . . . [and] their proposed solutions [to problems] are all based on 'apolitical' or neutral assumptions about society and in particular education's role in that society. (p. 98)

White (1982) comments:

> of all members of the teaching profession [the primary teacher] has traditionally been the least politically aware. Her typical milieu has been the world of art and crafts, of movement and drama, of learning to read and count. It has typically been a cosy inward-looking world, quite cut off from the complexities of politics. (p. 203)

In direct contrast to this ideology, those who attempt to address the problems of stereotypical practices and/or gender discrimination, by definition, set out to confront traditional beliefs and to politicize education. To those teachers who hold traditional beliefs and notions about society, this challenge will undoubtedly be seen as a threat, and what is seen as threatening is frequently reacted to with hostility. It is, therefore, not surprising that for the most part primary teachers are so resistant to addressing the issue of gender. Those who believe in the benefits of individual-istic child-centred approaches react with complacency. Others are threatened by what appears to be an attack on fundamental beliefs. How then will it be possible to achieve change in the attitudes of members of a profession which finds the issue of gender totally at odds not only with many of its members' personal beliefs but also with their concept of what is entailed in being a primary school teacher? Further, if the notion of equal opportunities is so problematic, how much more difficult will it be to ask the primary sector to address anti-sexist initiatives? If initial teacher education fails to provide opportunities for stu-dent teachers to challenge their attitudes to gender inequalities, it is perhaps not surprising that I, and other feminist teachers, find ourselves in the position of having to raise awareness amongst colleagues before any whole school policy can be effectively implemented.

Breaking the mould: suggestions for interventionist strategies within primary education

To achieve change in any sphere is often a long and painful process, but to alter the attitudes of people in an institution which is by its nature conservative and resistant to change is a process which is fraught with difficulty. It seems both from personal experience and from the findings of my research that, although it is over a decade since the passing of the Sex Discrimi-nation Act, the stereotypical attitudes towards gender of many teachers within the primary sector mean that the issue remains an optional concern, left to the interested few.

   Attempts to make consideration of this question a compulsory rather than an optional issue are problematic. Some commenta-tors suggest that moves towards compulsion may be met with resistance and a deepening of complacent and hostile attitudes (Whyte 1983b; Taylor 1985; Ord and Quigley 1985; Brah and Deem 1986). However, my argument is that to attempt to achieve change in a sector which has a particularly deep-seated resistance to gender, more is needed than the expectation that these issues will, through goodwill and consensus, gradually permeate through to become 'good primary practice'. My personal experience as a primary school teacher and my findings as a researcher lead me to believe that this is not happening and will not happen. What I believe is necessary to achieve change is a blend of an element of compulsion and skilful initial and in-service education to ensure primary practitioners 'own the change'. This could be achieved in a number of ways:

1 Policy guidelines, having been produced, need to be implemented and monitored. It is common practice for LEA advisers to visit schools to see, for example, good mathematical practice. So should they visit to see good practice in terms of gender differentiation? Without the 'top-down' support, those at the chalk face attempting to produce this good practice stand to lose credibility and, to lose heart.

2 Similarly, advisers with responsibility for equal opportunities might make suggestions that at least one of the Baker INSET (In Service Education of Teachers) days be devoted to gender issues.

3 Taylor (1985) has commented upon the necessity for INSET provisions being directed towards headteachers. Although those at the grass roots may struggle for change, little can be achieved without the support of those with the power to make key decisions. Such courses must then be followed up by the support of equal opportunities advisers and advisory teachers.

4 Policy can only achieve so much. However, measures such as these would give the time and space to those who have more in-depth knowledge of gender issues to engage in workshop techniques such as those used in World Studies Teaching (see Appendix 2). Those techniques are designed, through such means as discussion, games, and role play, to make issues personal to those taking part. These workshops could then be followed up by a series of staff meetings in which the issues raised could be pursued at greater depth.

Jayne (1987) has commented on the usefulness of such activities, but also states that to work successfully they require a climate of trust and co-operation. This climate can only be brought about over a period of time. Only if discussion and workshop time is given to gender will there be a chance that primary teachers will begin to take it on board as a personal concern and only then will they begin to own any strategies for change. All this is possible. However, it must be said that, in an educational climate which now has to come to terms with the priorities of a National Curriculum, what is more likely to happen is that gender issues in primary education will be destined to move ever more rapidly to an even more marginal position.

CHAPTER 6

'A Sort of Career': Women in Primary Schools

HILARY BURGESS

A 'career' has been defined as a 'course or progress through life or history; way of making a livelihood and advancing oneself' (Sykes 1979). Understanding teacher careers in the broad context of a 'life' or 'history' has been the focus of work with teachers in the secondary school (cf. Sikes *et al.* 1985; Ball and Goodson 1985). However, such an approach has rarely been applied to the study of primary school teachers where the predominance of women provides a new dimension to the study of careers. It is significant that the dictionary definition cited above also provides an explanation for 'career girl' and 'career woman' as being a 'woman who works permanently in a profession'. That such an explanation is necessary immediately suggests that there are two 'types' of women, those who have careers and those who do not, and it denotes a separation, therefore, between women's lives and women's careers. This chapter intends to focus upon the careers of women teachers in the primary school and to examine the gender-created gap between women's lives and careers. Such a task demands, in some respects, an autobiographical approach, alongside the work of others, as, having been a primary school teacher myself for fourteen years, I am better acquainted with my own life and career than that of anyone else! It is, however, a very selective account, within the parameters of this article, and as Graham Greene (1971) points out, an autobiography can only be 'a sort of life' because 'it begins later and it ends prematurely' (Greene 1971: 9). While my own work as a teacher in a primary classroom has ended, my career continues as a teacher in higher education. The constraints and ambiguities which I felt as a woman primary school teacher still exist and therefore I offer my own selective autobiographical account of 'a sort of career' in teaching to illuminate some of these issues. My own career is discussed alongside commentaries on other teacher careers. Any career, however, needs to be examined in the context of the work or profession in which it is located and so I shall begin by focusing upon the 'facts', ideologies and myths which surround primary education and primary schooling.

Rhetoric and ideology

The rhetoric of primary education and what it means to be a woman primary school teacher are inexorably intertwined as each presents an aspect of the teacher's role. However, the notion of primary schooling has fluctuated with the passing decades of this century. I will, therefore, focus upon two phases, primary schooling in the 1960s and in the 1980s, as these eras illustrate two of the major themes of primary education: child-centredness and pupil achievement.

During the expansionist optimism of the 1960s a child-centred ideology, where pupils learned through activity and experience rather than by rote and repetition, began to dominate the primary educational scene. Alexander (1984) suggests a number of reasons why teachers were, and still are in some respects, so eager to embrace a child-centred approach to teaching. He argues that the class teacher system requires teachers to be responsible for both the 'whole child' and the 'whole curriculum'. At the same time, the increased professionalization of teaching in the twentieth century has meant that teachers have had to justify their right to be professionals through expert knowledge and specialization. Alexander states:

> There was a need to develop a conceptual framework for the practice of class teaching which – whatever its educational benefits for the child – would support and sustain class teachers, provide them with a professional identity, and 'prove' that the approach with which they were saddled by virtue of historical accident was the best one from the child's point of view. Child-centredness, whatever its educational merits when examined dispassionately provided the best available ideology to meet the primary class teachers' situation. (1984: 14)

The class teacher system, therefore, both promotes and sustains a child-centred ideology. Within such a system, Alexander argues, there are only two roles which are significant, the head teacher and the class teacher. The introduction of a new salary structure for teachers in 1987, with the majority of teachers being on what is termed a mainscale, re-emphasizes for primary schools the separation between head and staff and works against the introduction of a clear management structure. Indeed, Alexander argues that the role of the head is one of 'paternalism' and represents moral authority within the school which, in turn, is supported by the maternalistic role of the class teacher, while Acker (1987) suggests that 'the family-image created by the male head/female staff might be better as part of the social reproduction process, as one way society perpetuates its gender divisions through models presented to young children' (p. 86). Each of these views on the organization of primary schooling suggests that there are clearly defined roles for male and female teachers, equating the classroom with domesticity and school management with leadership and power which have traditionally had a male connotation. This division of roles for men and women teachers is supported by official documents such as the Plowden Report (CACE 1967) in which headteachers are presumed to be male as 'his school' and 'his staff' are discussed. Such remarks are only the tip of the iceberg, however, where women and teaching are concerned.

The Plowden Report was one of the most comprehensive and powerful educational documents written on primary education. It was, and still is, regarded as a beacon for primary school progressivism and child-centred education and yet the forwardness in its thinking did little to help the status of women primary school teachers. Indeed, the differences between men and women teachers are highlighted in the chapter on 'The Staffing of Schools'. While the Plowden Report remarks that one of the great changes since the inter-war period is that women teachers no longer have to resign on marriage, it goes on to state, 'Wastage is a particularly serious problem for primary schools because so many primary teachers are women' (CACE 1967: 313). Furthermore, in discussing the numbers of male and female teachers in secondary, junior and infant schools, it comments, 'In infant schools in 1965 there were only 97 brave men out of a total of 33,000 teachers' (CACE 1967: 313). The proportionately different numbers of men and women teachers at all levels of primary education were noted alongside the numbers of teachers who held posts of responsibility or were heads and deputies. The findings showed that more than half the men but less than a quarter of the women held senior positions within a school. A major concern of the report, however, was to encourage married women teachers back into teaching by persuading local education authorities to create more part-time posts in primary schools. This was to be supplemented by in-service training for these teachers which would stress work with young children. Such recommendations made little impression upon the unequal career prospects for men and women teachers and, in some respects, helped to maintain the status quo where the management and organization of schools, classrooms and teachers were concerned. Women teachers, especially if married, were encouraged into part-time work with young children rather than into a career structure which would provide them with promotional opportunities.

These comments in the Plowden Report represent the educational rhetoric of the 1960s but how might this have changed in the 1980s? Here two reports are particularly relevant, *Improving Primary Schools* (ILEA 1985) and the Select Committee report *Achievement in Primary Schools* (House of Commons 1986). The first of these documents, more widely known as the Thomas Report, provides a detailed examination of primary schooling in Inner London. Two in-depth commentaries on the content of this report are given by Nias (1986) and Burgess (1986). Nias, for example, argues that it is 'deceptively orthodox' and that while there is little new or controversial in terms of curriculum planning, progress and continuity it is a radical document because of the ideological framework in which it is set, where working-class and multi-ethnic pupils are 'kept firmly in view'. Burgess focuses upon the curriculum and classroom practice and, like Nias, considers the recommendations for these aspects of primary schooling will only be effective if there is direct intervention by LEAs and the Inspectorate. Burgess also highlights how the lack of clear evaluative procedures for the curriculum may hinder the careers of women teachers as the route for evaluating the implementation of recommendations is to be included in the annual report to governors by headteachers. As Burgess (1986) points out:

Such views appear to endorse the status quo in primary schools which have a large female teaching force and a male dominated leadership . . . The suggestion of the Thomas Report to use head teachers as the group to report on development in primary schools will reinforce the position of male hierarchy. If the Thomas committee were sincere in their earlier proposals concerning class, gender and race they would have ensured that these groups were provided with a means of advancing their views. Accordingly, reporting procedures need to provide a structure whereby *all* teachers can be involved. On this basis, the perspectives of women teachers could be advanced in their own right rather than being subsumed beneath those of the male hierarchy. (p. 95)

While the position of women teachers may not be enhanced by the Thomas Report they are acknowledged, and the differences between the numbers of male and female teachers and headteachers is clearly illustrated by a table in the third chapter. This table shows the number of male/female teachers and male/female head teachers in Infant, JMI and Junior Schools in ILEA in January 1984. Such a comment cannot be made about the Select Committee report (House of Commons 1986) which takes a unisex stance and discusses neither men nor women teachers. This approach, which may have been an attempt to avoid discrimination between the sexes, like the proverbial ostrich, merely buries its head in the sand. A close analysis of the formation of the Select Committee which wrote the report and the witnesses who provided evidence reveals a number of interesting facts. The eleven members of the committee were all male and during the period July 1984 to June 1986 when there were changes in the membership, again no women were added to the committee. Furthermore, from approximately 180 witnesses who were invited to give evidence for the report less than a third were women. Is it not extraordinary that a report on primary education, where the majority of teachers are women, is written by a committee of men and most of the witnesses are men? The invisibleness of women in education has been well documented by Spender (1982) who also argues that knowledge is constructed by men:

Like it or not, we have to come to terms with more recent discoveries . . . that human beings invent or construct knowledge in accordance with the values and beliefs with which they begin. What knowledge gets made, and what does not, why and how it is used, can provide much illumination about the people who have made it and the society in which they live. If there is little knowledge about oppressed groups, and if what there is portrays oppressed groups as inferior or incompetent, then it is perfectly reasonable to assume that those who are making the knowledge are not oppressed, and that they are not particularly interested in challenging the basis of oppression. (p. 2)

To agree with this statement made by Spender has implications for the content of the Select Committee report which is heavily male dominated. It certainly raises the question of whose view and what kind of knowledge concerning primary schools is being represented? This is of particular interest where the ideological rhetoric of the Select Committee report is concerned when it discusses the 'achievement' of children as a key issue. Burgess (1988) has termed this the 'ideology of achievement' and considers the issues which this raises for primary education and the ways in which it is interpreted within the report. For example, 'achievement' is linked to many specific criteria: academic attainment, the application of knowledge, the development of personal and social skills and the motivation to persevere when faced with failure. All these criteria are well-suited to a subject-based curriculum and appear incompatible with a child-centred ideology.

Despite the opposing stances reflected within the Plowden, Thomas and Select Committee reports, the basic organization of primary schooling in a class teacher system is supported by all three documents and it is partly this which creates rigidity within primary schooling and maintains the familial notion of male/paternal head teacher and female/maternal class teacher. The ILEA document, however, does go some way towards breaking this pattern and outlines the negative aspects of the class teacher system as well as the positive. It also argues for a curriculum post to be included within each school so that staff might be able to develop their areas of responsibility more easily. These recommendations for curriculum co-ordinators are also echoed in the Select Committee report. Such changes, although not incompatible with the National Curriculum, appear to have become submerged under the debate surrounding educational issues such as the core curriculum and national curriculum policy, testing for 7 year olds, grant-related in-service training and 'Baker Days' to name a few, all of which have a high national profile. There does not appear, therefore, to be an opportunity in the near future to bring to the forefront of educational debate the anomaly of the roles which are created for and by teachers and how this affects the careers of both men and women. Having provided some of the ideological context and educational debate which surround primary school teaching, it is now possible to examine more closely some of the key stages in women primary school teachers' careers.

Career patterns

Women's careers in primary teaching are heavily influenced by the ideological assumptions about child-centred education which teachers themselves hold (cf. Alexander 1984) and by the organizational framework which supports the class teacher system. There are, however, other influences at work which may also affect the career development of primary school teachers, such as the romanticized notion of vocation, which can be seen as a vocation to being a 'class teacher' rather than a vocation to teaching as a career. The romanticization of primary teaching is eloquently captured by Steedman (1982) when she says:

> For women, however, there is the possibility of the romantic solution. Primary school classrooms are usually private places, rows of tidy houses strung along a corridor and a terrible intimacy grows there, six hours a day, eleven months a year. The clatter of the children may retreat, the room becomes a momentarily silent place, as if in a tank of water all the little fishes are strangely looking in from outside and there flashes the sudden, quick perception of oneself as a lonely, misunderstood martyr. The literature provides for this feminine romance, and school systems rarely discourage the eccentric, convinced, hardworking saint and martyr, for her labour comes cheap and lack of promotion is really what she expects. (p. 7)

This history of women in teaching is also closely linked with the familial aspect of primary schooling equating the class teacher with a mother, and here Steedman's comments on her own career in primary teaching (Steedman 1987) are illuminating:

> I didn't know this history when I entered that enclosed place, the primary classroom. I didn't know about a set of pedagogic

expectations that covertly and mildly – and *never* using this vocabulary – hoped that I might become a mother. And yet I became one, not knowing exactly what it was that was happening until it was too late, until I was caught, by the pressure of fingers, looks and glances. (p. 125)

When teachers enter a primary school and make it 'theirs' so that it is talked about in terms of 'my class' and 'my children' they also unknowingly support the career trap which prevents many very able women teachers from applying for promotion and maintains the notion of the class teacher as a 'mother'.

Interviews

The underlying pedagogic assumptions of primary education pervade every aspect of a primary school teacher's career. As a young teacher applying for teaching posts in a Midlands city I did not find it unusual to be asked questions in interviews which began with statements such as, 'When you decided that teaching was to be your vocation – how? why?' or, 'I see that you are married; will your husband mind if you take part in evening activities?' or, more boldly, 'Is your husband supportive of education?' All these statements and questions point out that, first, if a woman is in teaching it is because she has a vocation to teach rather than a wish to develop a career in education and, second, that she will need the support of a man if she is to adequately perform all the duties which the job demands. Since the 1975 Sex Discrimination Act gender-biased questions are rarely asked in such a blatant manner at interviews. However, evidence from teacher interviews in a comprehensive school (Burgess 1988) indicates that sexist questions are still asked in the 1980s.

Interviews can be regarded as a critical event in any teacher's career and, as Southworth (1989) points out, all interview candidates need to prepare themselves for both appointment and disappointment. He also suggests that those who are not successful should be offered career advice. I have on a very few occasions been offered 'advice' after interviews which has consisted of comments such as 'smile during the interview' which I felt hardly tackled the root of the problem as to why I had not got a particular job! There are also many women teachers who either do not regard their teaching career in the promotional sense or do not see it as an option which they are able to take up because of family commitments. Where a preponderance of such teachers exist in one school the staffroom can be a lonely and unsupportive place for a woman teacher seeking promotion. The kindest of comments might take the form of 'Well . . . if that's what you want – if you'll *really* be happy doing that', which all adds to the feeling that you as a woman teacher have 'no right' to expect a career which might take you up the promotional ladder and even beyond the classroom. These feelings are strongly endorsed when, as one woman teacher I worked with commented upon the appointment of a new headteacher, 'I don't mind who gets the job – so long as it's not a woman.' For this teacher apparently only a man could possess the abilities and qualities required to be a headteacher.

Critical phases in a career

The status of women in teaching has been well-illustrated by the career of Buchan (1980) who discusses her own career pattern in Australian schools. She examines the myth that teaching is 'a good job for a girl' and argues that if a woman wishes for more than just a job then opportunities are not available to her and the situation is very different to that of her male colleagues. Buchan comments upon her life as a teacher:

> At the end of 1977, I withdrew from teaching. I gave up my 'good job' and still think unkindly of the originator of the dream that 'It's a good job for a girl'. Until this myth is dispelled and the reality of teaching in a male-dominated school system is exposed, women will remain primarily in low-key positions or, like me, will withdraw to seek more rewarding and autonomous jobs. (p. 88)

Clearly for Lou Buchan working within the Australian state school system there were a number of phases and crises to her career which finally resulted in her resignation from teaching. Measor (1985) has discussed how the careers of all teachers go through similar critical phases when they are faced with choices and decisions. These she identifies as:

1 Choosing to enter the teaching profession
2 The first teaching practice

3 The first eighteen months of teaching
4 Three years after taking the first job
5 Mid career moves and promotion
6 Pre-retirement

(Measor 1985: 58)

While each of these events is a significant phase which all teachers may pass through, Measor recognizes that there are some critical phases within a teacher's career which are entirely personal, such as changing family circumstances or the death of a child or close relative.

One of the most critical phases of my career as a woman teacher is related to being granted secondment during 1982 and 1983 by the LEA which I worked for at that time. It is in some respects a very personal critical phase of my career although Griffiths (1986) has discussed the effect on teachers and their careers of secondments which enable them to follow a course of higher academic study. When I began the MA course in Curriculum Studies at the University of London, Institute of Education my original intention was to go back into teaching in primary schools and seek further promotion, which the added qualification of a Masters Degree would assist. However, having gained my MA and returned to teaching, I found that the qualification proved to be a hindrance rather than an asset. Indeed, I found that neither the LEA nor the headteacher of the school in which I worked were interested in sharing the expertise and knowledge which I had gained. I applied for deputy headships in the same area and my application forms brought a nil response, whereas only the year before I had been told by an adviser that I was regarded as being among the ten best candidates in the whole of the city who were applying for promotion. It was also passed on to me by a colleague that a group of headteachers who were seeking deputy heads had discussed the matter one evening at the local teachers' centre and one of them had commented, 'Do you know – I even had somebody with an MA apply for my deputy's job. I can't have anybody like that – I haven't even got a degree!' It was generally agreed among the headteachers who were there, and needed new deputies, that they too would not like to appoint a deputy head who was so highly qualified. These examples, and many others, made me feel that as a woman primary school teacher I had 'no right' to possess the qualifications I did and that there was no longer any room for me in the primary classroom. I had given twelve years of my life and my heart to many classes of wonderful children and the knowledge that I was no longer eligible for such a role was, for a long time, very hard to come to terms with. I briefly considered denying to myself that the year's secondment had ever happened and leaving my qualifications off my curriculum vitae when I applied for jobs. However, I decided that this was not an option I was prepared to take up and so left primary school teaching to pursue a career in higher education. A critical phase or incident, therefore, can have unforeseen and far-reaching consequences where a woman's teaching career is concerned. How, though, have those women who have achieved headteacher status managed their careers? (See Chapter 7.)

Evetts (1989) examines the career patterns of married women headteachers and the strategies which they have adopted. Here, she contrasts the way in which women headteachers have managed their career and family commitments. Evetts' exploratory study is of twenty-five women who were primary or infant headteachers, and who achieved promotion in the 1960s and 1970s. She identifies a range of strategies which they adopted during the course of their careers. These are, first, the 'antecedent career' where the woman is highly committed to her career and personal goals are secondary. Second, the 'two-stage career' where the woman is highly committed to career, marriage and parenthood and none has overall priority but there is constant negotiation and compromise. Third, the 'subsequent career', is the strategy adopted by women who placed family goals first and only thought about promotion when their home and families were settled. Evetts suggests that this option is the most socially acceptable and includes women who give up teaching to have a family and late entrants to teaching. Her final strategy she calls the 'compensatory career' and here the motivation for achievement is caused by personal failure in another sphere.

These women teachers had all been successful in achieving promotion and yet only those who followed the antecedent strategy might appear to have a career pattern similar to that of their male colleagues. However, as married woman teachers, their geographical mobility was restricted because of their husbands' jobs. Certainly, Evetts' work illustrates that women in primary teaching have to be prepared to adopt a range of strategies if they wish to follow a promotional career.

Conclusion

In many ways primary school teaching is regarded as a 'woman's job' and yet, to follow a promotional career within primary education can present immense difficulties for women teachers. Educational rhetoric as documented in reports by committees such as Plowden or the 1986 House of Commons Report has not regarded women in teaching favourably. Indeed, the Plowden Report (CACE 1967) considered married women teachers should be encouraged to do in-service work in the teaching of young children, while within the Select Committee Report (House of Commons 1986) women are simply invisible. The paradox of becoming a primary school teacher is, for women, a most extraordinary one. Women dominate the profession in terms of numbers and teaching experience and yet find it difficult to have a promotional career. Teachers' concepts about the ways young children learn and the class teacher system all work against the notion of women teachers performing any other role but that of 'mother' in the classroom. Of the small amount of research which has been conducted on teacher careers, Ball and Goodson (1985) make a number of investigative assumptions:

> First, that the teachers' previous career and life experience shapes their view of teaching and the way he or she sets about it. Secondly, that teachers' lives outside school, their latent identities and cultures, have an important impact on their work as teachers. This relates to 'central life interest' and commitments. And thirdly, that we must . . . seek to locate the life history of the individual within 'the history of his time'. (p. 13)

In the context of women primary school teachers' careers this set of investigative assumptions could prove very illuminating. The 'view of teaching' has, to some extent, been examined by Nias (1985) but this focuses upon teaching rather than upon examining careers in the promotional sense. Evetts' (1989) work on strategies of married women headteachers is the most recent although all her headteachers were appointed to posts during the period of educational expansion in the 1960s and early 1970s.

Women primary school teachers in the 1980s may have to use a different set of strategies in order to advance their careers. However, the context of women's careers will still need to be viewed as an aspect of 'life' and not simply as a job. Furthermore, the 'right' of women primary school teachers to achieve, to become highly qualified, to be successful needs to be examined as very subtly they are told not to be any of these things. The lack of promotional opportunity and the careers of women primary school teachers need to be put on the agenda of courses for intending teachers in universities and colleges and opened up for discussion among LEAs and schools. When the classroom practitioner, the women primary school teacher, can have a voice, and is listened to, then women may have the opportunity to develop their careers and be recognized as the major contributors that they are to the education of primary school children.

CHAPTER 7

Women in Primary Management

LESLEY HART

A young boy was tearing around the playground generally making a nuisance of himself. The headteacher of the school, who had a fearsome reputation as a strict disciplinarian, had made several futile attempts to get the boy's attention. Finally, the irate head managed to get hold of the boy and reprimanded him, starting with a question about why he had ignored such a potent voice of authority. 'Oh Miss,' he replied, 'I didn't realize it was you . . . I thought it was just a woman.' Being 'just a woman' can be a severe handicap in the world of education. My background as a teacher in the secondary sector had shown me that few women make it through the ranks to middle or senior management in secondary schools. But I naively believed, upon taking up my present post as teacher adviser for equal opportunities with responsibility for all phases of education, that primary education presented a different picture. I believed that women would have greater opportunities for promotion and posts of responsibility in primary education which has been traditionally the domain of women, with male teachers in the minority. However, as in most other walks of life, men seem to get further faster and more frequently than their female peers.

During the course of my research into this I interviewed a number of women headteachers from various authorities but, in particular, LEAs in the North of England. They represented a wide range of experiences, family circumstances, interests and aspirations. I also interviewed women deputy heads about their career aspirations, and discussed with governors, parents and pupils their views of women in primary education. The picture that emerged was depressingly familiar. Despite the impact of the Women's Movement in the last twenty years, legislation intended to promote equality of opportunity, and a growing awareness of the omnipresence of patriarchy, women do not expect to succeed as men do. Of the women heads I interviewed, all felt that they had achieved their positions more by good luck than good management; by being in the right place at the right time. Only one of the headteachers in my sample had entered the profession with any career plan in mind, and none of them had experienced systematic staff development or career appraisal as a matter of course. All felt that women still have to make a choice between career and family which men are never expected to do, and all felt that they were less confident than their male counterparts. It had also been made clear to some of them, when applying for promotion, that a man would be preferred. When asked about the kind of in-service training that would be helpful to women teachers, all except one of the headteachers immediately replied, 'Assertiveness training!'

It seems that women do not expect to succeed as men do; that they question their ability to do the job, and that they have to prove their worth before they are afforded the respect that men receive automatically. In order to understand the roots of these perceptions, I pursued two main strands of enquiry: how the women saw themselves as headteachers, and how they were treated by the people with whom they came into contact in the course of their work. Assertiveness training may be a valuable experience for women, but how effective is it if those in power view women as inherently inferior?

The career routes of the heads in my sample had often been determined by family circumstances. However, there were certain similarities in attitude and experience which were common to both married and unmarried women, parents and women without children. With one exception all the teachers I interviewed had a clear idea early in life that they would become teachers. In some cases this was expected because of family background, class and education, and the lack of other professional opportunities for women at that time:

> I came from a family where there were already two teachers and I don't think there was a lot of choice at the time because there wasn't much money around. Certainly, as far as coming from a big family, you were lucky even going to college. I fancied

teaching, but I think it was just that I was brought up in a teaching background.

(RC Primary Head)

One headteacher did not want to go into teaching, but parental pressure led to this:

> In some ways it was a deliberate plan in terms of my father's views. He was determined that we would have an education. I wanted to run a children's home, but to my father, if you didn't go to university, you went into teaching. When I got my 'O' levels I had such a shock that I'd passed them all, that I said OK. I went to college and didn't like it, but just loved my first teaching practice. So, in a sense it was lucky.

The appropriateness of teaching as a profession for educated, intelligent women does not rely solely on class or economic factors:

> That was all I ever wanted to do. I went home when I was four and told my mother I wanted to teach. I went to a private school and you either became a teacher, a nurse or a socialite. Out of my class, one became a consultant, one became a teacher, and the others achieved nothing.

(Primary head of a multiracial school)

Of the women in the sample who had children after they had started teaching, all took a career break. None anticipated returning to teaching, and all had due to financial pressure. Incidentally, all were married to other teachers. On returning to teaching, all these women found difficulty in securing permanent or full-time appointments, and so they experienced a wide range of schools because of a series of short-term contracts, supply teaching or experience posts. Although these experiences provided no security or opportunity for consistent staff-development, they were not necessarily disadvantageous:

> I did a year working in lots of first schools, which was an absolutely wonderful experience and gave me a great deal of confidence.

(Married primary head with one child)

A nursery head that I talked to achieved her present position by a most unconventional route. Having trained in primary teaching, she taught top infants for two years before leaving the profession to have children. She had no intention of returning to teaching. About ten years and three children later she became involved in running a play group. During the following seven years she attended numerous courses and earned great respect for her work. Problems with a very disturbed little boy in the playgroup led her to enrol on a university advanced diploma course on child development from birth to 13 years of age. All the other course participants were lecturers or teachers. She was the only person not working in mainstream education, was paying her own fees, and was generally referred to as 'the playgroup woman'. Her tutor suggested it was about time she returned to mainstream education, and, despite her initial reluctance, she went to see the LEA Primary Inspector. The Inspector asked her if she would like to participate in a joint experiment between the LEA and Social Services which consisted of placing a trained teacher in a social services nursery.

This experience was a baptism by fire. There was suspicion on the part of the nursery workers at a so-called education expert being drafted in, and an awareness on her part of the lengthy gap since she had worked in schools. Gradually respect grew for her work, and after two months she was visited by the Primary Inspector who suggested that she might apply for a post as a teacher/adviser. She felt a reluctance to do so as her secondment to the nursery had not long started, but also she felt her recent experience was irrelevant. However, she did agree to apply for a post at a new nursery school being built in the authority. The two posts available at that time were head and deputy, so she applied for the deputy post. When she took her application form in to the education offices she was told that the head would be appointed first. The clerk suggested she might apply for that, 'Nothing ventured, nothing gained.' On the spur of the moment she filled in another application form. She was interviewed for the post. Her opposition was tough, she had had no previous experience of interviews, and was amazed to get the job.

All the heads I talked to who had experienced a career break felt that they had reached their positions by irregular routes. They felt a little disorientated by not having had the same career progression as many of their colleagues. Some felt a lack of confidence in themselves, and in the way they were viewed by others who had followed more typical career routes.

Apart from my head and my husband I've had no support or guidance. I still have the hang-backs from my childhood when I felt, 'No, I can't do it.' And inside I get annoyed with myself because I think that's ridiculous. To some people I seem confident, and perhaps that's the real me. But inside I don't feel it.

(Primary head married to another primary head)

One woman felt it was an advantage to be older as you were more likely to be accepted. She had started her training when she was 30, got a teaching post, taught for a comparatively short time, and then become a head. However, in that comparatively short time, she did a university advanced diploma, a BPhil, and then had a year's secondment studying community education in another part of the country. Her late entry into the profession after family responsibilities had eased had enabled her to concentrate on her career:

It is easier for women to get promotion if they're old when they come into the profession. It's more threatening to see a young woman coming in and rocketing through, than it is to see an older woman.

There was a clear consensus amongst the women I interviewed that it is difficult being a young woman making her way through to headship. Younger women experience more suspicion, patronizing attitudes, and still have the conflict between parenting and working:

I feel sad about some younger women who, to get promotion, feel that they have to sacrifice their personal lives, which men never seem to do.

One young headteacher in my sample was the only one to have a career plan. On the way to achieving her objectives she had made decisions which few men would ever have to consider:

I've done all this with a partner I've never married. I haven't married, in a way, because he might be able to make more legitimate demands on me. Yes, there has been a sacrifice because you have to give so much time to it. I don't have children. That wasn't a conscious decision, I just suddenly realized time's gone, and there's still so much to do. There isn't a night during the week when I don't do two or three hours' school work. My partner accepts that, and I couldn't do the job with any less time devoted to it.

Childcare is not the only constraint on professional women. In a society where people are living longer, it is again seen as the responsibility of women to care for the elderly. The deputy head of the young headteacher quoted above has such responsibilities. She is an extremely conscientious, committed teacher with a well-earned reputation for never being off school. Her head-teacher had to order her to go home when she arrived for work whilst suffering from double pneumonia. Women are particularly sensitive to accusations of missing a lot of time because of family commitments, and they are reluctant to stay off even when quite unfit for work:

> My deputy – well, I don't know how she copes. She has a mother of ninety who lives with her, a husband, a big house, she has no assistance in the house, and a son.

The deputy in question told me:

> If one of them says, 'I'm ill,' in the morning, my tummy gets knotted up because I think, 'What will I do if I'm called home?' If you're committed to a profession you can't be staying off. I think that if I'm a deputy, that would be awful enough, but I couldn't say that I could be a head when I've got those commitments at home.

Her headteacher commented that she gives as much time and commitment to the school as the head herself. Her commitment, managerial skills and worth are obvious. However, her home circumstances have pre-empted any ambition to take her career any further. She also feels that she has reached her present position by being in the right place at the right time, rather than any inherent worth on her part.

All of the headteachers who have husbands or partners felt that their support had been a vital factor in their career success:

> I think a big influence in my life has been a husband who is proud of me, who is delighted in my success, who has supported me in childcare and has taken his role fully as a father.

Those married to teachers did not feel that their husbands felt any rivalry or jealousy at their success:

> All that time when I was going whizz, whizz, whizz and he wasn't, he was so supportive and proud of me. He made my life such that I could concentrate on school. He says that I'm married to it.

This woman had had a career break, had taken numerous supply jobs, temporary and experience posts on returning to work, and had a difficult struggle in becoming a head. She initially returned to work because of financial need.

Although they said that they had received invaluable support from their partners and that their success had not been resented, there was still a protective anxiety for their partner's ego:

> My husband and I were both acting heads, and when the jobs came up we both applied for them. I got mine and he didn't get his. That made me feel very guilty because I just felt it is wrong, which is nonsense. But he then got a headship within a month, so that it didn't really matter. I hadn't applied for as many jobs as he had. I'm still of the view that I have worth . . . now that he's settled in an adviser's job, now I can start. When he said, 'If something comes up for you, and you want it, go for it and I will then follow.' But I couldn't do that.

She had had a career break to have children, had followed her husband's career around the country, had returned to work because of financial pressure, and had returned by the usual circuitous route of low-status, impermanent posts. Her husband has now moved to another part of the country to take up a post. She is looking for appropriate positions in that part of the country.

The reasons that these women sought headships fall into two main categories; a desire to accomplish more in terms of educational practice, and applying for headships after a period as acting head, often during the merger of infant and junior schools. Some of them felt no real ambition until they compared their careers with those of colleagues:

> We had a male teacher who came to us on an experience post for a few months. He was seen to be charismatic and he got a deputy headship. And then a colleague down the road was applying for a deputy headship, and I thought, 'My God, if they can do it, I can!

Another head who had envisaged becoming a headteacher changed her mind after a period as an acting head. Two-thirds of the heads I interviewed became heads after being in an acting position. None felt that this had been good training for headship. Some had seen the position as that of caretaker because of their head's secondment, retirement or the planned merger of schools. None of them felt, therefore, they had any autonomy to lead the schools in new directions. The woman who lost interest in becoming a head after being acting head did become a head, though still feels uncertain of the correctness of that decision:

> Basically I allowed my ego to overcome my good sense because I was told, 'You will be meeting people getting headships and you will know that you are the equal of those people, and you will feel resentful that they have gone forward for it and you haven't.

Although none of the headteachers felt that they had been groomed for headship through systematic staff development, most felt that they had received encouragement from either working with a head who had encouraged them to seek promotion or encouragement from a sympathetic LEA Inspector. However, some faced great opposition in their search for promotion.

A scale two teacher with responsibility for the infant department of her primary school decided to seek a deputy headship. She found her male headteacher totally unsupportive.

> The reference I got from my head I wouldn't have given a cat. I was damned by faint praise, and I had worked damned hard. For a scale two I was doing head of the infant department, all the requisitioning, I had written the curriculum document that he was supposed to write for the LEA, and I had made or collected forty costumes for the school play. When I asked him about my reference he said that he thought I was far too nice to be a deputy head, and that he had to think about my marriage because he thought it would break up if I got promotion. He said that he was talking to me as a friend, a father, a brother and so on. I felt I was in a paper bag, and I was just battling and battling. It was very traumatic, because in those days I wasn't very assertive.

This particular woman is most emphatic that she would not have been able to succeed without the support of her husband and his pride in her achievements. The Primary Inspector intervened and secured her a scale two experience post for a year at another school:

> I shall always be indebted to the Primary Inspector because she did so much for me. So I came here and found the place absolutely wonderful. My female head gave me a permanent scale two within three weeks. By the start of the next term I was acting deputy head; two terms later I was the deputy head; a year later I was acting head. Then two years later, after the merger with the junior school, I got the lot.

Before the transfer to this school she had twice been interviewed for deputy headships. On returning to her school having not been appointed her head told her to 'stop playing around and get on with the job you're paid for'.

Another teacher who had had a very wide experience of the different phases of education, but who had concentrated on primary education, was encouraged in her career by her male head, but ran foul of the local authority. She had taken up a post in a newly established primary school. The head had decided that he would appoint his deputy from among his staff after they had worked together for two terms. Before this could happen he became seriously ill and called upon this woman to be acting head. She performed the job for two weeks until the Deputy Director of Education turned up without warning, demanded the school keys and handed her responsibility as acting head to a male member of staff. There was no criticism made of her performance, it was simply seen as a more appropriate responsibility for a man.

On her head's return she was duly appointed deputy, at which point her male colleague 'downed tools' and ultimately left. Her head later encouraged her to apply for headships, and on her second attempt she was appointed head of a primary school within the same authority.

In certain cases it became apparent that interviewing panels preferred to appoint men. Even after the Sex Discrimination Act some women were victims of clear discrimination when applying for promotion:

> When I went for a preliminary visit the female headteacher was quite open about wanting a man. I don't think she said it in so many words, but you understand these things. I had a super interview, but I was more or less prepared. The chairman of the governors very kindly rang me afterwards and said that the head had wanted a man, but I had got down to the last three, and due to the fact that she wanted a man, I was dropped. I wasn't bothered about that, I was just pleased with what I'd done.

Sometimes women heads are particularly keen to encourage other women to seek promotion, but meet with reluctance from governors, and a lack of confidence from women colleagues. One woman head was seeking a deputy:

I was given lots of advice. One headteacher said, 'What you want is a nice, young man.' At the end of the day the governors said, 'Well, it's so nice for you to have a man.' I'd appointed three scale threes who were all women. He got the job because, in the governors' opinion, and in my opinion, he was the best. But I'm sure the fact that he was a man influenced the decision. When I wanted a deputy there was a woman teacher I knew and respected and wanted for my deputy, but she wouldn't apply. I'm sure the governors thought, 'It would be nice for her to have a man for discipline.'

The headteacher of a school in an area of great social deprivation became head after a period as acting head during a merger. She feels that her relationship with her governors is excellent, but they had been hesitant in appointing her:

I think my governors were probably apprehensive about appointing me because they thought it was too tough a job for a woman.

All the heads I interviewed felt that they had the respect and support of their governing bodies, but that this had been earned consciously by their performance in the job. The same was true of all their professional relationships. Particularly persistent is the myth of male supremacy in the field of discipline. Governors are not alone in believing this; many teachers, parents and pupils hold the same view. There are, however, certain consumers of our educational system who do not agree with this.

Michael, a 10-year-old pupil who has recently moved from a primary school with only one male member of staff to a middle school with a lot of men teachers, told me:

Women teachers are best. They're nicer and fairer.

When he was about to move school a 'naughty boy' in his class was envious that he would be taught by a number of men at his new middle school:

He said that he liked male teachers better. He's always been [sic] a hatred of women teachers. He said that male teachers didn't seem to shout as much as women teachers, and that female teachers weren't as strict as male teachers. He quite liked strict teachers, and said that all soft teachers were stupid.

Michael continued to affirm his preference for women teachers because they were more consistent in their treatment and expectations of their pupils. In his experience the male teachers had shouted more, and for no apparent reason. He felt that if you were nice or nasty to women teachers they responded in the same day, whereas the male teachers he had experienced had lacked consistency.

Michael's comment about his classmate's prejudice is most perceptive and touches the nerve of the problem. In our society women are viewed as inferior and have to work extremely hard to prove the contrary. When they achieve this, they are merely viewed as exceptional, the exception that proves the rule. In my own teaching experience I have encountered Michael's classmate's view from pupils again and again. I was the form teacher of a particularly wayward class of 11 and 12 year olds who had just transferred from primary to secondary school. The class was two-thirds boys, and was dominated by a group of eight demanding boys. Very soon after their entry to the school they were proving to be a problem. They were fortunate in being taught by a number of strong women teachers, but their behaviour was causing concern. I discussed this with my form and was told by Matthew, an articulate and popular spokesperson of the form:

> Miss, it's because we've got no respect for women teachers. We behave for Mr — because he's hard and shouts at you, so we're frightened of him.

By half-term Mr — had a riot on his hands in lessons, whereas the children were responding well to, and enjoying their lessons with my female colleagues. My intention is not to imply that women are inherently better teachers or disciplinarians, but to question the belief that men are.

A mother I interviewed expressed her concern about her son moving from the female-dominated world of primary education to the male-dominated secondary sector:

> One of the nice things, as a parent letting your child loose on the world, about primary education, is that the female environment seems a very personal one, very secure. Although I'd like to see more men involved in primary education as I think it's good for children to have contact with both men and women, because it's female dominated it's got a character that's different from the character of a middle or high school, and which at that point in their lives is quite secure for them. What worries me is the

transition from that secure, female-dominated situation where people are allowed to relate to each other on a very personal level, where the way people feel, talk and what they care about matters, to a competitive, dog-eat-dog atmosphere.

Another parent spoke of her concern for her daughter aged 9 who is bright, confident and assertive. Her male teacher seemed to find this threatening in a girl, and viewed her genuine enquiries as a potential undermining of his authority. A head and her woman deputy found that their relationships with parents caused them concern. They had taken up their posts following a school merger. This had taken place at a particularly difficult time during teacher action, when many parents were finding school closures during lunchtime and other such sanctions were causing inconvenience, difficulty and concern:

> I think that every single relationship my deputy and I had for the first two or three years were filled with anguish and horror. We blamed ourselves in relationship with parents; we regarded everything they brought forward as legitimate criticism and it was only after they'd battered the hell out of us that we suddenly realized, 'My God, no matter what you do you're not going to please these people.' I think we both had a woman's instinct for smoothing the way and sacrificing ourselves, offering ourselves up as doormats.

It would seem that one of the most important lessons to learn is to have confidence in your own abilities. Not only do women need to prove their worth to others, but they need to prove it to themselves. This affects their relationships with their staffs and has implications for their management styles. All the heads felt that they had to win the respect of their staffs by having firm ideas of policy, but they wanted to be facilitators in a democratic process of determining policy rather than be dictators. All felt uncomfortable in their role as head when this involved criticizing colleagues, and felt that the key to successful relationships with their staff came from standing up and being counted:

> In the beginning with your staff you have to establish that you're going to stand up and be counted when they need you to do that. I think that some people think that it's a weakness to have a democratic style of management. I don't always take what they say, but I always listen to what they put forward. It's not unique to women, this style of management, but the tradition of a

woman being the carer, the one who makes things easier, the peace-maker, is a good one, as long as you've got principles behind that.

The principles for being a good headteacher seem to be the same for being a good teacher of any sort; leading the horse to water and leaving it to discover the best way to drink for itself.

> Pulling a staff together is a bit like guiding an elephant. It takes some getting moving, but if you can be really courageous about it, once it starts moving, all you have to do is sit on the top. The one mistake you can make is to sit back and think that you've done it. I still think that the best leader is the one of whom people say, 'Well, she didn't really do it anyway – we did.' And they feel they are in control, which they are. I'm just guiding the elephant along.

Headteachers, in the course of their work, have dealings with numerous outside agencies such as school doctors, dentists, social services, the police and building workers. Some of the most overt sexism that the heads I interviewed had experienced came from visitors to the school. There was general agreement that not only do women have to put up with sexist behaviour which their male counterparts would probably never experience, but also male heads get more immediate attention to such things as building work, whilst the women are fobbed off:

> Oh God, I don't even say my name when I ring the buildings section, they know my voice. In the end I ring up the contractors myself in the holidays and get them out. There's no other way.

One head always anticipated difficulties with workmen:

> I bristle really with workmen because I go in expecting to be treated like a little, whimsical bit of a thing. So I go in fighting and being fairly authoritarian.

The treatment they received varied from being patronized because of their sex and/or youth, to actual sexual harassment:

> When we sometimes feel we're not getting anywhere on changing staff attitudes to Equal Opportunities, we suddenly realize how far we've come when people come in from outside and they're appalling. The delivery men who came the other day looked at me and said, 'Any chance of a cup of tea, dear?' I just didn't know how to react to that. So I said, 'I'm the headteacher, I'll get my

secretary to get you one.' (great laughter) And only afterwards thought that was just as bad.

Comments range from amazement that young, attractive women are headteachers – 'They didn't make headmistresses like you in my day!' – to sexist comments about other women heads being 'a bit of all right'. Harassment does not stop at words:

> The dry rot man today was just about to pat me on the bottom when I said, 'Are those your vehicles in the yard? Would you mind moving them as they're going to be a hazard to the children at home time?' Then he realized that I had some authority. But he was about to have an entirely different conversation with me.

I doubt if any male head has had that to contend with.

Are there any advantages in being a female headteacher? The main advantage seems to be a closeness that is possible with mothers, particularly Asian mothers and women who are single parents. A headteacher of a multi-racial school commented that:

> I have a lot to do with mums. They will come and talk to me about their periods, their marital problems, you name it and I get it. I think it's particularly important when you get lots of mums on their own. Now maybe my male deputy head could do that . . . but men find that much harder.

This was the only advantage that was given in response to my question!

The final question I asked was about appropriate training for women teachers. Apart from the obvious need for assertiveness training, it was generally felt that it was important to give women time, encouragement and praise:

> We've got to be given a little bit extra time. We're talking about centuries of culture which have made us the recipients of things rather than the 'doers'. So the first thing is masses of assertiveness training.

Anxiety was expressed that such things as local financial management of schools might militate against the appointment of women heads; that women might feel reluctant to take on yet more responsibility, and that they might be viewed as less competent than men in handling finance. One head felt that it was still a man's world, and that to succeed in it women have to adopt men's tactics:

I think there should be more women involved in appraisals, management training etcetera. We've got to be geared into a male way of working through the system. A man teacher comes in, and really, to some extent expects promotion. He expects there's going to be a route and a structured way through. Women often come in because they want to work with children, or it may be a second income, but they're not expecting anything back.

The themes constantly running through the responses to my questions were that women are always striving to prove their worth, trying to improve their practice, questioning their ability and assuming blame, and smoothing the way for others. One head felt that women need help to overcome the constraints of such conditioning:

Assertion training and things that help women raise their self-image; stress management so that you can set yourself realistic goals and not expect perfection.

After concluding these interviews I was left with mixed feelings. In one respect I felt profoundly depressed that there were still so many battles to be fought and won, and that we had made so little progress. On the other hand, I was left with a feeling of hope that change will come through the efforts of women heads such as these who are striving, not only in their professional lives as women, but as teachers with a vested interest in equality of opportunity for their pupils.

Reluctantly, I'll leave the last word, yet again, to a male. In a discussion with a 9-year-old boy about women bosses, he asked, 'Can a man become Prime Minister?' Perhaps change is coming.

Acknowledgements

I would like to express my gratitude to all those who assisted with this chapter, but particularly to the women headteachers who gave their valuable time, advice and shared their experiences.

Policy and Practice

CHAPTER 8

Equal Opportunities in Leicestershire

JOHN GIBBS

During the spring term of 1986 I was seconded by the Leicestershire Education Authority to direct an action research project examining Equal Opportunities (Gender) in primary schools in the Melton Mowbray and Vale of Belvoir area. This involved working in twenty-two primary schools with numbers on roll ranging from sixteen to five hundred. As Leicestershire schools have traditionally enjoyed a large degree of autonomy in comparison with those in many other LEAs, a school-focused action research method was favoured rather than a 'top-down' model. This chapter concentrates on the findings of the research project and is a commentary on that rather than on the implementation of any LEA policy. The main areas which emerged from the project and which will form the basis of this chapter are: the reactions of headteachers and staff to the project; INSET (In-service Education for Teachers) work in the project schools; work carried out with children; how the approach used in the project influenced organizational and attitudinal changes in the schools. Finally, some indication will be given of the extent to which the project influenced the development of equal opportunities policies in several schools. Before examining these factors in detail, I think it is important to provide my personal perspective on the situation in Leicestershire regarding equal opportunity initiatives at the time of the project.

By January 1986 Leicestershire County Council had issued an Equal Opportunities Policy Code of Practice to all establishments under its jurisdiction. The purpose of this code was to give practical guidance to promote equality of opportunity within the LEA for all employees and potential employees, irrespective of their race, ethnic origin, religion, sex, marital status or disability. A working party of the council had produced a Report on Multicultural Education in 1984. The LEA already employed an adviser for multicultural education and also resourced and staffed a Multicultural Resources Centre. As far as gender issues were concerned several initiatives had already been undertaken in the primary and secondary sectors although these had been on an *ad hoc* basis. A discussion document entitled 'Women Teachers and Lecturers in Leicestershire' had also been produced by the LEA. In addition, the WEEL (Women for Educational Equality in Leicestershire) Group had established a resource bank of equal opportunities materials with a grant from the Schools Curriculum Development Committee. My own interest lay in a belief that it was important to offer to the children in our primary schools an education which allowed their development as individuals rather than as members of a gender grouping. Having been involved in a pilot project in 1985, I was invited by the LEA to develop the work further in the 1986 spring term.

The reactions of headteachers and staff to the project

The project was both a continuation and an evaluation of a six-week pilot project undertaken twelve months earlier. This initial work had been carried out in primary schools with predominantly white school populations in the Melton Mowbray and Vale of Belvoir area and was specifically concerned with raising awareness amongst teachers of some of the main issues of sex discrimination/differentiation and its effects on pupils' later choices and achievements. The reactions of headteachers and teachers to the project varied enormously. At an initial meeting for headteachers to discuss the project in the first week of the 1986 spring term, eighteen of the project's twenty-two schools were represented.

At this first meeting ten out of ten female headteachers and eight out of twelve male headteachers attended. A number of doubts were expressed about the timing of the project which coincided with initiatives on primary science and multicultural education but, overall, the headteachers were enthusiastic. The LEA's carrot of a small injection of capitation to each project school was very well received! At a lunchtime rendezvous to discuss the meeting in a local hostelry, a sign which read 'We don't serve women here, you have to bring your own' acted as an appropriate reminder of the need for the initiative.

Having explained the aims of the project to the headteachers involved, either at the meeting or by telephone to those unable to attend, I then made appointments to see the headteachers individually in their schools. All twenty-two headteachers agreed to this one-to-one meeting at which I negotiated when to visit their school to see the staff. All but one of the headteachers then allowed time for me to see the staff. Each of the schools distributed a questionnaire on staff attitudes to gender issues in schools which was to be used for discussion purposes at the subsequent staff meeting. However, whereas most headteachers allowed access to staff, a number put up some obstacles which made it rather difficult to undertake in-depth work with the teachers. For example, although many of the headteachers provided time for an introductory session at a staff meeting – either lunchtime or after school – one headteacher refused access ('too busy'), another allowed contact with staff only by letter ('to gauge whether there is any interest') and a third head only permitted contact with his staff after he had undertaken a complete review of what I was going to do with them. Interestingly enough these headteachers were all male . . . although I would, of course, hesitate to state whether this had any bearing on their decisions!

Other headteachers allowed the use of supply time which had been allocated to all schools in the project for an in-depth introductory session with their staff. The use of this supply time is detailed later. Given below are a number of comments made by headteachers on my initial visits. I think these quotations speak for themselves:

Male: I feel money could be better spent.
Female: I agree with equal opportunities in theory but it makes me mad when I want to appoint a man.
Male: Equal opportunities is important because it is the law.
Female: The junior boys always put the PE apparatus away for the infants because they are stronger.
Male: Boys do not answer the telephone or make coffee because they would rather be outside playing football.

Having made contact with all schools and arranged to see the staff in all but one of them, the next stage of the procedure was

the introductory session with the staff. At this session I employed
a number of key strategies. In the first place staff were asked to
treat the subject in an open and professional manner and to
consider the educational implications for the children in our
schools. A discussion took place focusing on literature and
research articles on the subject. The tape/slide 'Triggers for
discussion' was viewed and posters and booklets produced by
the EOC (Equal Opportunities Commission) were on display.
Finally, the results of the questionnaires distributed earlier
were examined. The reactions of the teachers were varied. Some
members of staff were very interested, others were apathetic and
a minority were hostile to the whole idea. It was noticeable that
the less enthusiastic the headteacher was ('I'm not a chauvinist
but . . .') the more hostile members of staff were. There appeared
also to be a feeling of being 'set up' in one school when the whole
session was received by a staff of six teachers who were very
frosty and sarcastic. The apathy and hostility were not necessarily related to the sex of the teacher as a number of female
teachers were also unreceptive. Additionally, many male staff
were extremely receptive and interested in the issues raised.
Below are some comments made by the teachers:

> *Male*: I don't want women to become too masculine.
> *Female*: There is a danger you have to think every time you speak
> to children.
> *Female*: I think women should be taught to look after men.
> *Female*: Does this mean you would allow boys to come to school
> in dresses?
> *Male*: I think women with children should stay at home and look
> after them.
> *Female*: But boys are different from girls!
> *Female*: I like men to be men and women to be women.
> *Male*: Girls are not insured to play football.
> *Male*: But surely boys and girls have to be separated in the
> register?

Given the mixed reactions which existed amongst headteachers
and teachers, INSET work required careful and sensitive
planning.

INSET work in the project schools

Supply cover to release teachers was an integral part of the project and it is possible to identify seven major ways in which the time was used by the teachers:

i   to attend an 'awareness raising' session as described earlier
ii   to visit colleagues in classrooms and other schools
iii to make visits to outside agencies
iv to analyse reading and other curriculum materials
v   to develop strategies and devise curriculum materials for promoting equal opportunities
vi to withdraw small groups of children
vii to examine literature available for teachers

Schools were encouraged to work on areas of interest to themselves. As the project continued a number of schools began work on equal opportunities policy statements and some of these will be examined later.

The INSET work was primarily school focused as can be seen from the following accounts written by teachers involved in the project. These accounts demonstrate how many schools came to recognize the extent to which gender inequalities pervade the primary school curriculum.

School A

'The teachers at the school did not feel they were sexist originally! The discussions, though, did heighten awareness of certain organizational practices and casual remarks which may exacerbate bad practices at home and in the media. The initial introduction did not achieve its aim of drawing a large staff together on the problem. Fortunately, follow-up visits on a one-to-one basis linked with specific areas of development within the school did the trick. Staff, in conjunction with their investigations into multicultural education, are looking closely into the hidden curriculum, organization, resources, curriculum, and role models.'

School B

'I have to admit that when the idea was first raised I was sceptical that there would be nothing in it for us as I thought that we were as even-handed an any teacher/parent can be . . . On reflection I realize how erroneous that view had been. Research which I conducted with my own class using a tally system indicated and agreed with research elsewhere that boys get a disproportionate amount of my time and attention.'

School C

'We decided to pay a visit to the Literacy Centre for the purpose of appraising new material with a view to purchase. The exercise was far more time-consuming than we had expected. Further, it was to a degree depressing to find when perusing new schemes, it was all too often bright new icing – but same old cake inside. Ultimately, we were left wanting a more meaningful, varied and interesting reading diet for our children. We planned:

1 To enhance and extend our reading resources
2 To be very careful and selective about reading matter offered to our pupils – interest being paramount . . .'

School D

This school produced a model of how their supply time was used (see Table 8.1).

School E

'Supply cover in our school has been used as follows:

1 Three full days so that each member of staff (six) could spend half a day with you on your introduction to the project
2 Three full days so that infant staff could individually pursue their own topics within the project
3 Three full days so that Junior staff could meet to discuss an Equal Opportunities statement and policy.

The above extracts are just a few of the INSET initiatives undertaken by teachers in the project schools. As already stated, much of the supply cover was used for working with, and observing, children and these initiatives will be examined in the next section.

Table 8.1

Drama	Attitudes	Play
Drama as a medium for equal opportunities awareness	Examining our own attitudes (whole staff approach)	Life in the play corner. Observation video or sound taping. Possible place of teacher interaction

Feedback from each formulation of policy statement for school

TV Programmes	Books	Curriculum Issues
Looking at TV programmes for role stereotyping. Letters from children to be sent to TV companies.	Sex stereotyping in whole area of books; fiction, non fiction, maths, etc.	Children's attitudes to work. Working with children, encouraging children to observe and comment. Looking at ways of raising awareness.

Work carried out with children

There is little doubt that work carried out with children in the classrooms of the project schools and the observations made proved to be very valuable and worthwhile, as well as extremely revealing. It will be difficult to do justice here to the variety of approaches attempted by teachers and for detailed descriptions of children's work it is necessary to read the full report of the project (Gibbs 1986). However, I will attempt to pinpoint some examples of children's work which seemed to typify the approaches used. Much of the work undertaken in classrooms during the project consisted of attitudinal studies whereby children were asked to depict people in various occupations either in pictures or in words. One group of seven children aged 4 plus were asked to draw a picture of various people in certain occupations. This task was given without any previous discussion and the results were very much as I had expected. All seven children portrayed the doctor, dentist and police officer as male and the nurse as female. Six of the seven children drew a female hairdresser, whilst the shop assistant was seen by the children as being both male and female. There were one or two drawings in which I was unable to determine the sex of the person drawn so I asked the child concerned to give the person a name. To my own horror, when asking about the doctor I said, 'What is *his* name?'!

Other examples included work with children who were asked to write about how they viewed being a boy or a girl and their views of the opposite sex:

- I like being a girl because I get earrings and presents like that. Girls are neat and tidy. Girls can wear dresses and boys can't.
- I am glad that I am not a boy because they cannot wear skirts, dresses and trousers but girls can.
- I don't want to be a girl because they have to wear skirts and they play with Sindies and Barbies.
- I like being a boy because boys play Star Wars and A-Team and Knight Rider and Air Wolf.
- I don't want to be a girl because girls wear dresses and they wear necklaces and they like playing with dolls and they like doll stories.
- I am a girl because I like boys. I would like to be a boy 'cause they can play rugby and girls don't like playing it 'cause it is a rough game. I like being a girl because you get nice clothes.

A number of teachers commented that after doing work of this nature with children they realized just how important it was to devise a strategy for equal opportunities and often the work was followed by discussion to ensure a more 'unbiased' viewpoint. Another popular strategy employed by teachers was that of discussion. Consider this report by a member of staff engaged in the project:

> I asked a group of 6-year-old boys and girls why they were boys and girls, what it was about them that let me know that they were boys and girls. We first discussed the physical difference of boys having a 'willy' (their name for it) and girls having different bits which raised a few giggles but that was the only difference specifically mentioned. I deliberately did not suggest anything else so I could find out what would come from the children. I then asked them if they were of the opposite sex what they thought they would do or how they would behave in such a circumstance. They were asked to paint a picture of themselves doing some-

thing they thought only girls or boys would do. My conclusions were as I had suspected that most of the children have their expectations and notions of their parents and peer groups. They were a bit surprised by the questions at first and it raised quite a lot of discussion amongst themselves. I don't believe many had ever thought about it before.

When the work was finished we sat in a group to discuss it and look at the pictures. It then occurred to some of them that both boys and girls can do all of the things mentioned. One boy said, 'There is a girls' football team,' and another said, 'You can play with my Star Wars figures.' They were interested for some minutes in the discussions and after coming to a general decision that sex stereotyping was somewhat 'outdated' (of course not in those terms) they were ready to listen to a story which they had chosen previously.

There were also many examples of observations of groups of children and audio-taped discussions. Both the observations and tape-recordings demonstrate children's own entrenched stereotypical attitudes. Given below is an example of a discussion a group of children had with their class teacher. The children are between 8 and 10 years old:

Teacher: Which games do you like to play in the playground?
Girl A: American football! I've never actually played it though.
Teacher: Do you think you should be allowed to when you're older?
Girl A: Yes.
Teacher: Do you think there might be a problem?
Girl B: No. As long as they let girls play.
Teacher: What do you others think? Should they let girls play rugby and football?
Boy D: I'm not really bothered.
Boy C: I think American football's for boys really.
Teacher: Why?
Boy C: Girls . . . when you play American football with all the big shoulder things, girls don't have really big shoulders. When they get all jumped on they start crying.
Girl A: Not always.
Boy C: The thing girls should be is where they have those big fluffy balls. That's more realistic for them than playing the game.
Teacher: Oh you mean Cheer Leaders.
Boy C: Yes, I just think boys are better than girls.
Teacher: In what way?

Boy C: Well, boys can do better things than girls.
Teacher: Tell me what things.
Boy C: Er . . . they can play football better than girls, throw
snowballs better than girls and make snowballs better than
girls and . . .

How the approach used in the project influenced
organizational and attitudinal changes in the schools

It was possible to detect organizational and attitudinal changes in
the schools by employing three main methods. Firstly, there was
a questionnaire distributed to all members of staff in the project
schools. Secondly, as a number of the schools had been involved
in a pilot project twelve months previously, it was possible, by
re-issuing the questionnaire in the pilot schools, to contrast the
results with those 'new' to the project. Finally, the headteachers
of the pilot study schools were asked to complete a questionnaire
detailing changes in their attitudes and the organization of the
school, if any. Although a degree of caution must be attached to
the interpretation of the results of the first questionnaire on
account of the relatively small number of staff involved, nevertheless the results proved heartening. They appeared to indicate
that the level of awareness in the pilot study schools was
significantly greater than schools new to the project. Additionally, although the answers to the follow-up questionnaire
were subjective and should be interpreted accordingly, the sample indicated that school staffs were treating the subject
seriously. Detailed results of both questionnaires appear in
Appendix 1.

The project's influence on developing equal opportunities
policies in a number of schools

Although the aim of the project was not specifically to help
schools formulate equal opportunities policies, a number of
schools took advantage of supply cover available to do exactly
that. Mention has already been made of one school's whole
school approach. Another school produced a policy statement
for the school brochure:

The School seeks to develop positive attitudes of behaviour appropriate to living in a multicultural society and positively seeks to promote a respect for the individual, regardless of race, creed, colour or gender.

A third school devised a statement for the school brochure and also produced a policy discussion document which set out the following strategies for promoting equal opportunities:

1 We must endeavour to provide equal opportunities for boys and girls as far as is reasonable in *all* aspects of the curriculum eg. science, CDT, games and PE.

2 We should avoid grouping children according to gender. In our view this often happens in the following ways:
   (a) coat peg allocation
   (b) register listing (alphabetical or chronological alternatives)
   (c) lining up
   (d) seating arrangements
   (e) generally in the organization of lessons eg. PE

3 We should have realistic (pragmatic?) examination of curriculum material for bias (possibly with particular reference to reading schemes).

4 We ought to make a conscious effort to administer the same pattern of rewards and punishments to both boys and girls.

5 We should encourage equal responsibility for tidying, cleaning and caring tasks in the school.

6 Encourage girls as well as boys to take part in more physical tasks such as moving chairs, tables, sandwich boxes, etc.

7 Observe the roles that children adopt in play or drama activities.

8 Involve all children in all types of creative work eg. cooking, needlework, pottery.

9 We should think carefully about the question of male courtesies to females and decide whether this might perhaps be broadened and viewed simply as part of a wider responsibility for courtesies to all others eg. why not hold the door open for any person not just a woman? This will certainly need further discussion.

10 We recognize that our own behaviour and attitudes as teachers are important as role models.

11 We feel that there may well be many occasions when we have to make a positive intervention and perhaps draw particular

attention to some inequality, but our hope is that much equality of opportunity will come about quite naturally and unconsciously.

Two other schools developed equal opportunities discussion documents, and by the time the project had come to an end, one of these schools had succeeded in obtaining the support of all staff and governors for the implementation of its equal opportunities policy document.

Conclusion

The results of the project enabled a number of conclusions to be made:

- The project raised levels of awareness significantly.
- There was evidence of organizational changes in a number of schools.
- Supply cover proved to be an important factor in the development of the project and was used in a variety of interesting ways made possible by the action research method employed on the project.
- It became clear that the injection of extra capitation for purposes of developing curriculum and teaching materials is vital.
- Interest shown in the initiative varied but the vast majority of schools involved undertook an encouraging amount of work and treated the project in a thoroughly open and professional manner. A minority of schools were not so enthusiastic. These all had male headteachers! At the same time, several male headteachers were as enthusiastic as the female headteachers.
- Complacency is the biggest enemy of equal opportunities, particularly in a number of schools with male heads. The reaction of a number of colleagues emphasized the emotive nature of this subject.
- Visiting the schools was much more effective than arranging centrally based courses, in my opinion. Many colleagues commented to this effect.

Postscript

Two years on from the project I still have fond memories of the visits I made, the reception I received from colleagues in schools and the privilege of visiting many different classrooms and staff-rooms. I also realize that, as a male headteacher, I was received rather differently than other colleagues would have been and that, anyway, it could be argued I am not able to perceive problems in a subject which is fundamentally about the female position in society. However, I feel that the project proved valuable, not only for the schools involved – and a reading of the full project report is evidence for that – but also because I realized that I had not grasped the full implications for my own teaching/leadership role in school. I mean, it's not very good for the soul to realize that the only male teacher in the school is white, middle-class and yourself – it's a poor equal opportunities role model!

Since my project, the Leicestershire approach to gender issues has, in my opinion, been modified. Twelve months after the project there was another one in Loughborough area primary schools. This proved to be the last *ad hoc* project and Leicestershire has since appointed an advisory teacher for equal opportunities. In addition, the advisory service in the LEA is currently being restructured and one area that an adviser will have responsibility for is equal opportunities. The equal opportunities resource bank mentioned earlier has grown enormously. There have also been many courses for teachers of all age groups who are interested in gender issues. As well as this, one Leicestershire group of the PrIME (Primary Initiatives in Maths Education) Project is examining maths and gender. This group has already conducted workshops on gender issues and is currently compiling a handbook. I feel that initiatives such as these with practising teachers examining the issues and designing materials for use in the classroom within the context of a whole school policy is where the future success of equal opportunities initiatives lies.

CHAPTER 9

Leeds Primary Needs Programme and Gender

DENISE TRICKETT

Leeds City Council has adopted a policy of equal opportunities for woman and men, girls and boys. However, whilst the authority has a general policy on equal opportunities relating to all departments and aspects of council work, it has, as yet, no specific policy referring to education. This situation seems to be common to many LEAs. More recently, however, because of the importance of education in council services, many authorities, including Leeds, are recognizing that an equal opportunities or anti-sexist policy for education may be necessary.[1] It is not enough though for an education authority to produce such a policy, unless it is prepared to help schools and other education institutions implement it:

> Transformation of policy into practice is essential if girls and boys are to receive an education that is genuinely anti-sexist and anti-racist. (ILEA 1985)

Too many policies are unread, or disappear in the system, and therefore become meaningless token gestures. Implementation of the policy means monitoring and evaluating it. This must be built into the policy so that positive changes and improvements can be made as mistakes are recognized, and concerns and priorities change with time.

This chapter describes the background and development of equal opportunities and anti-sexist initiatives in primary education in Leeds, and how a general equal opportunities policy for the whole Council is being applied to education. It describes how the initiative first began, the strategies used for development and some of the problems faced by those involved with this work. It examines how progress has been continually monitored and evaluated, and changes made accordingly. Finally, it talks about the current situation and the possible future development of equal opportunities with the authority.

In the beginning . . .

In September 1986 Leeds Education Authority established the post of an 'Equal Opportunities Support Teacher for Girls and Boys' in primary education. On starting the job, I received a letter from a governing body in the area:

> Both headteachers were adamant that such a policy (i.e. equal opportunities) had been carried out for years and we failed to see the necessity of a special teacher being employed to oversee this function in primary school . . . the Governors felt that whilst there were shortages of teachers unnecessary positions should not be created . . .

A nice welcome to a new job!

After two years of committed work by a number of people, equal opportunities for girls and boys has become part of primary education in Leeds. It is an area of education in which schools and staffs are aware, but do not always show a positive attitude. Some teachers recognize the importance of the issue, others remain indifferent, and still others are firmly entrenched in their traditional ideals. But whatever the reaction, gender issues in primary education are no longer hidden.

The establishment of the post of Equal Opportunities Support Teacher

Equal Opportunities in Leeds began as part of a programme implemented by the City Council to enhance the quality of primary education throughout the city. The Primary Needs Programme (PNP) was introduced in September 1985. Around 350 additional teachers have been appointed to assist in programmes of curriculum and staff development. A new Primary School Centre and a Multicultural Resources Centre were established to provide additional facilities and resource bases for in-service activities for primary teachers. Extra nursery nurses and home-school liaison assistants as well as support teachers and co-ordinators for equal opportunities, science, technology and mathematics were appointed. The 'real' initiative to include equal opportunities within PNP came from the council's Women's Committee. At a special meeting to discuss education, the Women's Committee commented that 'the promotion of equal opportunities for girls' had been excluded from the PNP initiative. Given that the broad aim of this programme was to meet the educational needs of all children within the authority's primary schools, it was vital that any inequalities in terms of sex differences were not overlooked. As a result of the concern expressed by the Women's Committee, officers from the council's Equal Opportunities Unit and the PNP discussed ways in which equal opportunities could be integrated within the Primary Needs Programme.

In April 1986 the Education Committee finally approved a project on equal opportunities for girls and boys, to be encompassed in the overall aims of PNP. These aims were as follows:

(a) to develop in each primary school a non-sexist learning and social environment
(b) to actively encourage implementation of anti-sexist practices in primary schools
(c) to ensure that the full potential and abilities of both girls and boys are fully recognized
(d) to end stereotyping in both curricula and non-curricula activities.

In order to co-ordinate the project, a small officer group, to include representatives of PNP and the Equal Opportunities Unit, was to be established. A senior primary teacher on secondment (Equal Opportunities Support Teacher) would be responsible for its implementation and provide support and assistance to primary schools as necessary.

Structure of the Equal Opportunities Support Group

Whilst gender issues in primary education were being given some recognition and a post of Equal Opportunities Support Teacher established, at this time no similar initiative was taken by the authority to do the same in the middle, secondary and tertiary sectors. There was, however, some agreement that a comprehensive, coherent strategy for promoting equal opportunities across all educational institutions was eventually necessary, and the authority has been working towards this over the past two years.

In 1986, then, equal opportunities in education was a new venture for Leeds, and I, as Equal Opportunities Support Teacher, started from a very uncertain, fairly isolated and lonely position. In line with the proposals agreed by the Education Committee a small group (the Equal Opportunities Support Group) was established to alleviate this isolation and co-ordinate the implementation of the project. The Support Group was chosen by the co-ordinator of the PNP, the Women's Officer from the council's Equal Opportunities Unit and myself. The underlying criteria behind the decision of who to include in the group were, firstly, to have a range of people from all sections of primary education in order to give the project credibility and status, and secondly, to include those who had already shown an active interest in equal opportunities work. The structure of the group was finally agreed as follows:

Co-ordinator of the Primary Needs Programme
Senior Primary Adviser
Head of Primary School Centre
Women's Officer (from the Council's Equal Opportunities Unit)
One Advisory Teacher
One Headteacher
Two Teachers
The seconded Equal Opportunities Support Teacher

The way forward for the Equal Opportunities Support Group

The terms of reference of the Support Group, agreed at the first meeting, were to implement the aims of the Primary Needs Programme in relation to equal opportunities. The group set out to do this by discussing a strategy for development over the initial year. A planned co-ordinated approach was seen as preferential to working in an *ad hoc* fashion, which would have been frustrating and unstructured. The group aimed to be as realistic as possible in its goals, recognizing that this was a long-term project; sexist attitudes and practices within schools could not be eradicated overnight. Specific priorities were identified by the group. These were: INSET work on gender issues in education; school-based projects; building up a resource collection and assessing other LEAs' approaches to equal opportunities. The implementation of these would run parallel to each other and they were all seen as equally important in raising awareness in equal opportunities within schools. These priorities would be monitored and evaluated by the Support Group at regular meetings, so that progress could be assessed and changes in organization and approach made if necessary.

Publicizing the Equal Opportunities Support Group

In the first few months one of the main priorities for the Group and Support Teacher was to publicize the issue of equal opportunities within primary schools, so that teachers and staffs would be aware that the authority had undertaken such a project and that an Equal Opportunities Support Teacher had been appointed. This was done in a number of ways. A short information sheet on equal opportunities was sent to all primary schools, offering help, advice and support to those schools that were interested. An article explaining the initiative was written for Leeds 'City Scene', which is the newsletter the council delivers free to every household in the area. Also a display was mounted at the Primary School Centre where I was based, using information mainly from the Equal Opportunities Commission, and non-sexist, non-racist story books suitable for the primary age range borrowed from the Education Library Service.

At the initial meetings of the Support Group various questions raised their head which had to be answered. For example, what terminology should be used – 'equal opportunities', 'anti-sexist', 'non-sexist'? Would schools understand these terms? Should schools be asked to write an 'Equal Opportunities' policy? Should 'guidelines' be imposed on schools? What could be done about those schools that expressed no interest or even hostility? We recognized that the issue of sexism in education is a political minefield, whilst at the same time agreeing that it should not be. All children should have the right to achieve their full potential, whether they are girls or boys, and if for any reason, whether on the grounds of sex, race, class, disability or sexuality, they are not doing so, then the authority has a legal and moral obligation to do something about it. The Group accepted the sensitivity of the initiative, recognizing that many teachers would be unaware that a problem exists, or misunderstand the issues involved. Initially it was agreed that 'Equal Opportunities' was a more acceptable term to use than anti-sexist education, even though anti-sexist education must be the aim, and was stated as such in the aims of the Primary Needs Programme. There was total agreement that 'guidelines' should not be imposed on schools, but that awareness should be raised by the implementation of the priorities outlined. Guidelines would not be written until 'Equal Opportunities' was established as an acceptable part of educational practice. Because of the size of the project to be undertaken (there are 238 primary schools in Leeds) it was decided to concentrate on those schools and staffs which expressed some interest in equal opportunities work. From this, positive discussion and ideas would filter through to others, and therefore more schools would become interested and take up the initiative. This is, in effect, what has happened over the past two years, but there are still some schools that have chosen to ignore the issue. The Support Group is very aware of this, but we believe that as awareness of gender issues in education increases, and positive changes are made towards good practice, the area of influence will be extended. Eventually, however, tackling those schools which refuse to acknowledge that a problem may exist will have to be faced.

INSET work

The INSET programme has been one of the most important aspects of the initiative in raising awareness of equal opportunities and anti-sexist education. Courses and discussions have been centre-based and also school-based. Some schools are now using their training days to look at this issue.

Centre-based initiatives – 'top down' approaches

Centre-based introductory courses on gender equality are repeated regularly, and these are followed by a more detailed course of practical application for those who want to study the issues more deeply. These courses have been offered to all primary teachers, including headteachers. Training has mainly been on the basis of increasing awareness of sexist attitudes and practices within schools, stimulating discussion and making suggestions for change. An anti-racist perspective underlies all INSET work. More specifically, the courses have looked at:

i   what sexism in the wider context of society and equal opportunities really means
ii how schools reinforce sexist attitudes and practices, mainly via the hidden curriculum, for example, school organization, classroom interaction, books and resources, curricula activities etc.
iii positive ideas for change and suggestions for good practice, for example, assessing where a school is starting from, raising awareness with teachers by monitoring free choice sessions, looking at children's favourite toys etc.; projects to encourage children to question and challenge traditional sex stereotypes.

Headteachers of all the schools involved in the first phases of the Primary Needs Programme, and Primary Needs Co-ordinators (i.e. senior teachers assigned to particular schools to initiate and support school-based development and curricula work) have attended sexism and racism awareness courses, which have been run jointly by the Multicultural Advisory Teacher and myself. Similar courses have been organized for Primary Advisers and Advisory Teachers, some deputy headteachers, probationers, Home-School Liaison Workers and Primary School Centre Staff. INSET work needs to be followed up, so that schools and teachers can implement the ideas raised by the courses in a meaningful way. If follow-up work, help and support is not available, then it is likely that some schools will be unable to progress.

As Ord and Quigley (1985) have pointed out, teachers who demonstrate a commitment to equal opportunities can easily become marginalized and experience feelings of isolation. To attempt to overcome this an Equal Opportunities Working Group, open to all primary teachers, has begun to meet on a regular basis. This group provides an opportunity for teachers to come together to share their concerns and problems, and also discuss ideas for anti-sexist work in their classrooms and schools. The group has in effect, changed its focus over time. Now, as well as acting as a support group, it is a much more positive working group, initiating projects itself. For example, the group is largely responsible for writing and producing an equal opportunities news-sheet, that is distributed to all primary schools once a term. The news-sheet is an important way of spreading information and contains articles about teachers' own experiences in the classroom, ideas for good practice, cartoons and future events. Response has often been positive, with other teachers and schools enquiring about in-service courses and training sessions. It has, however, produced negative responses, such as, '. . . appears to advertise fairly often propaganda courses about equal opportunities and gender issues. These seem presumptive and unjustified . . .'

This group has also become involved in writing to publishers of reading schemes asking about their attitudes and policies on sexism in books, reviewing a number of children's books, and taking photographs of children in non-stereotyped roles.

As well as the Equal Opportunities Working Group, a group specifically looking at mathematics and gender has been set up. This was in co-operation with the PrIME (Primary Initiatives in Mathematics)[2] Co-ordinators. Again the group is open to all interested teachers. One of the priorities for PrIME has been to look at equal opportunities in relation to mathematics and a teacher was seconded for one year to work with the group to produce an in-service pack. The pack documents all the issues around girls and mathematics and suggests ways of running centre-based and school-based in-service courses. These are being piloted in a number of Leeds schools. The group is now focusing specifically on construction materials, looking at why girls are less confident in using such equipment than boys and suggesting strategies for improving this situation by planning a sequential development for spatial ability. A small group of teachers are also looking at gender issues and the computer.

Centre-based approaches: one school's response

One school, in a policy statement on 'Sexism and Gender Issues', gives some indication of their process of development:

The impetus
An in-service course organized by the LEA and run by a seconded teacher was attended by the headteacher and this gave the initial impetus to the school's commitment towards a policy of equal opportunities. Following this two other members of staff attended similar courses and staff discussion was set in motion.

The method
As with all curriculum development within the school framework, the whole staff were involved. The members of staff who led the discussion initially tried to present the existing situation dispassionately. Arguments were backed by research and not clothed in emotive terms. Initial reactions were mixed. Some staff members rejected the validity of the concept citing the ideas as another form of extremism or merely the latest educational fad. Others were bemused or pointed out that they had survived the educational process and life without damage. Some were disinclined to commit themselves but an atmosphere for discussion was established. Two further meetings were generated from this initial input. By the end of the third meeting the idea had gained validity and was accepted as a matter for serious concern.

As the idea of gender issues became established as a topic for serious discussion, staff became aware of situations, attitudes and classroom practices which all reinforced sexual stereotyping.

The result
How to tackle these issues became the next area for discussion. At first, perhaps brought on by embarrassment or a feeling of unease, the subject was treated in a somewhat frivolous way. Jokes and comments about gender issues became the apparent order of the day. Although initially very worrying we soon realized that this was a reaction to their own stereotyped attitudes, both as teachers and members of society. As the humour of the situation subsided a new awareness emerged which was illustrated by unsolicited apologies for unguided remarks and practice, and positive moves to enforce a policy of equal opportunities were set in motion . . .

The Governing Body of the school has also been very much involved in the school's progress towards equal opportunities and has contributed to the policy statement:

We were very pleased to find out that the decision makers in the school valued the idea of positive action and were keen to motivate other members of staff towards a similar approach . . .

Obviously not all schools and teachers attending INSET courses have been able to follow-up the ideas in such a productive way. Many teachers talk about their isolation in school, how they are made to feel 'silly' and put down because they express an interest and are concerned about sexism in education. This is another problem the Support Group is aware of and is trying to alleviate. It has been discussed with the Primary Advisers and Advisory Teachers so that they can offer support and assistance to individuals within schools and can also point out and encourage headteachers to understand the validity of equal opportunities work. Supportive structures must be available otherwise the individual teacher can become very frustrated and demoralized.

School-based projects – 'bottom-up' approaches

Another priority of the Support Group was to involve interested schools in specific projects relating to equal opportunities. A pilot scheme was set up in three schools, but others have followed up in-service training in this way.

All schools taking part in such projects have had an initial input from me, so that all the staff have at least participated in an introductory discussion on gender issues in education. One or two teachers within each school have been given the responsibility of co-ordinating the project and liaising with me. The basic aim of the projects was to raise awareness on equal opportunities by identifying any inequalities in terms of sex differences within the school and discovering the contributing causes. If inequalities were found to exist, then the school discussed whether changes in practice and/or organization were necessary, and if so, what strategies would be most effective to produce change. The projects were, and are, continuing to be monitored and evaluated by the school and the Support Group. In the long term, examples of good primary practice in relation to equal opportunities in one school can then be documented and shared with others.

Schools have approached the projects in different ways depending on their starting point and according to their needs and individual situations. This has meant that in some schools all teachers have been, and are, involved in research and observation skills, in others it has involved the staff of a particular age range. However, whatever way the projects have been organized, any findings and suggestions for future developments have been referred back to full staff meetings, so that the whole school can participate in further discussions and are completely aware of what developments are taking place.

One of the initial schools involved in the pilot project looked at 'free choice' activities. Three teachers from different age ranges observed 'free choice' sessions for half-hour periods over a number of weeks. The objective was to monitor groups of children to establish whether there were any differences in the choices made by girls and boys, and to see if there were any differences in the way girls and boys played: for example, did children play co-operatively or particularly quietly or boisterously? The observations did reveal that stereotyped play was taking place and that this was more marked as the children got older. Monitoring also showed that certain groups of children were using the same materials and equipment over and over again, and were, therefore, getting very little experience of a wide range of activities. After a productive meeting to discuss these findings, the staff discovered that there were a variety of ways of organizing and structuring 'free choice' activities to ensure a more equal access and experience to all children. The suggestions made have, for example, been to ensure teachers understand the value of play and how equipment can be used to its best advantage, the sharing of ideas, and the importance of teachers participating in activities. These ideas have been useful as examples to other schools.

Another school, also in the original pilot scheme, developed in a different way:

> The need to look at equal opportunities arose out of two concerns. The first was our recent awareness of cases of child sex abuse, and the need to help children understand their right to say 'no', the second because of growing concern about behaviour in school, particularly in the playground. We focused on the disruptive or aggressive behaviour from some boys, and the difficulties some girls experience when trying to deal with this.

The school decided to investigate three main areas relating to equal opportunities, in order to discover whether there was a problem. The areas of concern were:

(a) The Playground – to try and establish the causes of disruption, and whether there actually are differences in play between boys and girls
(b) Book Resources – to investigate the extent of sex stereotyping evident in our book resources, particularly the core reading scheme
(c) Free Choice Activities – to investigate boy/girl choices of play activities within the classroom.

At the end of a year's project the teachers within the school had become much more aware of sex differences in education. The reading scheme was eventually changed, and although this was not solely because of stereotyped images in books, it was recognized that it was an important influence. After finding stereotyped results in relation to 'free choice' activities, a design and technology project was established to ensure girls' familiarity and confidence with construction materials. The projects are still continuing in the school.

Whilst the two pilot schemes outlined have initially been with raising awareness amongst teachers, other schools have focused on encouraging children to question and challenge traditional sex roles of men and women. One school, during 'Book Week' in Leeds, looked at the invisibility of women and girls in children's story books. On counting the number of images of males and females, the classic response from the boys was, 'Oh great, we're winning!' A sensitive teacher pointed out the implications of this, and opened up discussion with the children on the importance of equal opportunities. Again, these findings were reported back to a staff meeting for further discussion.

School-based projects have obviously been different in each school, but the work has often been supplemented with displays, governors' meetings and parents' meetings. A copy of 'Genderwatch' (Myers 1987) has been given to all schools participating in the projects, so that the co-ordinator has a valuable reference whatever aspect of the school curriculum or organization is being looked at. The projects have been frequently discussed by the Support Group, who have made valuable suggestions for change in terms of new activities and new directions in which work can proceed.

Resources on equal opportunities for girls and boys

A Primary School Centre was established as part of the Primary
Needs Programme in 1985 as a base for INSET work and to offer
'good' resource facilities for primary school teachers. Before this
date there was no central resources pool available to teachers in
Leeds on the subject of gender issues in education. The Support
Group, therefore, made it a priority that resources be collected
and displayed at the Primary School Centre. This would help to
publicize the importance of equal opportunities and to supplement the INSET courses, and also aid teachers in their understanding of the issue and with their work in the classroom. There
is now a large collection of resources available which is continually being expanded. This includes non-sexist, non-racist books
for children, information books for teachers, LEA documents,
pamphlets/news-sheets from the Equal Opportunities Commission, photopacks, lesson plans, and videos. The resources can be
borrowed and many teachers, schools and students make use of
this facility.

I, as Support Teacher for equal opportunities, am based at the
Primary School Centre and am thus able to deal with enquiries
from teachers and schools as necessary. Informal discussions
with teachers, whilst time-consuming, are extremely important
in raising awareness of gender issues.

Contact with other local education authorities

The final priority of the Support Group in the initial stages
of work was to ascertain what progress other LEAs had made
towards developing equal opportunities in primary schools, for
it is possible to benefit from their good practice and learn from
their mistakes. I visited various authorities that were prominent
in this work, including ILEA, Brent, Newcastle, Humberside,
Sheffield, Wigan and Bradford. What was apparent from the
discussions with other authorities was the wide variety of
approaches adopted to implement equal opportunities in
schools. Some LEAs had a policy on equal opportunities or
sexism in education, and had inspectors or advisers working
on this issue; some had seconded teachers working on specific
areas of equal opportunities, some had asked all schools in the

authority to write a policy, and others had made guidelines available to schools. Most, however, did not have anyone working specifically in primary education.

The visits were of great value, ideas for INSET work and resources were collected, and the problems and mistakes made by others honestly admitted. The feeling came across that those working on gender issues within authorities were totally committed to their work, wanted to share information and help if they could, as well as make progress wherever possible. Sifting through all the information was a difficult task for the Support Group; some ideas were adopted and others were left aside. This process led to a more comprehensive strategy of development being worked out, that was relevant to the situation in Leeds primary schools. The visits to other LEAs also progressed in another way. In conjunction with the Adviser for Equal Opportunities from Bradford and Equal Opportunity Officers from Wigan, a conference was organized for those women working on equal opportunities from LEAs in the North of England and the Midlands. The conference enabled us to share our experiences and a network and support system was established between those present; it is proposed that a conference will be held on a yearly basis.

The current situation

During the two years that equal opportunities has been on the agenda in primary education various inroads have been made. One such attempt to raise awareness of the whole area of sexism in education was undertaken by the council's Women's Committee. The committee, in association with the main teaching unions, organized a conference entitled 'Women, Girls and Education'. This was well attended, with over 150 women and girls present. As well as being informative, the conference aimed to make recommendations and proposals to appropriate bodies and set up support groups and networks as necessary. Although the conference was not aimed specifically at primary education, most of the workshops were relevant. These included child abuse, girls and technology, governors, male violence, black women in education, and promotion prospects. A workshop specifically on issues in the primary sector was held and again important links were made between members of the Support Group and teachers and parents. The workshop recommended a number of points, three of which the Support Group is discussing and considering:

1 After two years of work on equal opportunities in primary education should all schools now be asked to have a policy?
2 Should there be compulsory training for all headteachers?
3 How do we get all the school community (supervisory staff, secretaries, governors etc.) involved in training?

The conference was an important addition to the work being undertaken in primary schools. Because of its success officers of the Women's Committee and Education Committee are now looking at proposals for a follow-up conference for both men and women.

The Support Group has met every six weeks since the initiative began. Two members of the group (the Senior Primary Adviser and the Co-ordinator of the PNP), after eighteen months during which they saw the project off the ground and established as an integral part of primary education, had to leave. They have been replaced by an Adviser for Primary Education who has been given specific responsibility for equal opportunities, and an officer from the Policy and Co-ordination Unit within education. The Support Group and I have co-ordinated all the initiatives outlined and maintained an overall view throughout. We have tried to monitor progress made, and to work out future developments and new priorities.

Evaluating change and progress on equal opportunities within primary education is an extremely difficult task – it is very hard to measure changes in attitudes. The Support Group has to some extent been assisted in this task of evaluation by the Primary Needs Independent Evaluation Project (PRINDEP) at Leeds University. This project is evaluating the whole of the Primary Needs Programme. After two years PRINDEP have published a report on *Defining and Meeting Needs* which includes a review of equal opportunities in Leeds Primary Schools (PRINDEP 1988). This outlines the provision, the support and resources that are available, some of the limitations of the equal opportunities project, and suggestions for further progress.

Some general statements on the progress towards equal opportunities and an anti-sexist learning environment within primary education in Leeds can be made. All primary schools in Leeds must be aware that gender issues in education are being taken seriously by the authority. All schools receive news-sheets about equal opportunities in education and are aware of all in-service training courses relating to this. Advisers and advisory teachers, and staff at the Primary School Centre have attended an in-service course, and are supporting initiatives in schools and asking questions at interviews. Some headteachers and teachers are very involved and supportive of equal opportunities, and are trying to raise awareness and promote change within their schools. Some teachers are working on individual projects in their classrooms and some are participating in working groups. The links and networks developed between all these schools, advisory staff and teachers are of the utmost importance in raising awareness and spreading positive information, and by doing so have increased the supportive structures that provide confidence and assistance to teachers and schools. In more practical terms in-service training courses are continuing and developing. Assertion courses for women teachers are now being run, and self-defence courses, also for women teachers and girls, are in the discussion stage. School-based projects are continuing and the number of schools involved has increased.

The collection of resources and display at the Primary School Centre is now a valuable asset in the promotion of equal opportunities and is being used much more widely by interested people in education. Contact with other LEAs is being maintained, and acts as an important resource for the Support Teacher.

However, despite all these positive initiatives the Support Group recognizes the fact that combating sexism in education is a huge task. Implementing equal opportunities for all children will be a slow process, but is one to which the Support Group is totally committed. It has been this commitment and work by the Support Group that has ensured that some changes have taken place in the promotion of equal opportunities in primary education in Leeds. Without that Group one individual or seconded teacher could have done very little.

Leeds Education Authority is now in the process of developing a new structure for equal opportunities so that an overall coherent strategy is applied to all sectors of education. The initiatives taken in the primary sector will be integrated into a more positive and more effective strategy, so that improvements made in the primary area will be fully reinforced and continued in the secondary and tertiary establishments. Only a systematic tackling of the issues within all sectors will bring about the changes necessary to ensure that all children will have the best opportunities for their educational development.

Notes

1. How an authority approaches the issue will depend on its political make-up and the will and understanding of its members. For a fuller discussion of the differences between equal opportunity approaches to education and anti-sexist education see Weiner (1985).
2. PrIME is a national project and was set up in 1986 under the directorship of Hilary Shuard at Homerton College, Cambridge.

CHAPTER 10

Inside the Lego House

ELIZABETH BURN

I have been a primary school teacher in Gateshead and Newcastle Upon Tyne for thirteen years. Typical of many women with children, combining family and work commitments has meant that I have moved up and down the career ladder. In the North East of Britain, shortage of permanent posts has resulted in many women with children finding great difficulty in re-entering primary teaching. So, when I examined gender issues at primary level I discovered that it was not only children's opportunities that appeared to be limited. Women teachers, especially those with children, have been discriminated against and wastage of ability has affected women staff as well as girls in our primary schools (see Section Two). This chapter is written from a personal viewpoint and is concerned with research I carried out in four primary schools in 1986–87. The impetus for the research stemmed from my involvement with Newcastle's Sexism in Education Group. The Group was formed to look at classroom practice and was made up of both primary and secondary teachers.

I started to attend the meetings of the Group because it had become obvious that, in my classroom, girls and boys behaved differently, were treated differently, and had different expectations of school. Girls generally appeared to like school, they conformed and were seen as 'good' and willing to help. On the other hand, boys were often in trouble, especially at lunchtimes, more likely to present learning difficulties and to be seen as trouble-makers. My own experiences as a parent also made me aware that girls and boys were expected to conform to certain stereotypes and this limited their opportunities. The meetings discussed resources used and attitudes expressed, and we recognized a need to make our authority aware that sexism interfered with the good primary practice we were attempting to achieve. Meetings were held in local schools and by 1986 a temporary Teacher-Adviser with reference to gender was appointed. It was clear that research needed to be carried out in Newcastle schools and I was offered a two-term fellowship at Newcastle University. Two terms are hardly enough to become familiar with the issues and to carry out research unless one already has a background that includes some knowledge of gender stereotyping. Since I had completed an Open University course concerned with women's issues and studied for a Diploma in Advanced Educational Studies, I was regarded as a suitable choice. Also, as a classroom teacher, I would be seen as having credibility and knowledge of routines and practices in schools. The fact that I am a woman would allow me to blend into the female-dominated primary school; I would be less conspicuous than a man and also less of a threat.

I approached the fellowship well aware that I had to find the most productive way forward and with the intention of producing materials for future INSET (In Service Education of Teachers) work. It was a priority that I used the talents and knowledge that many women primary teachers have, but lack confidence in expressing. Walden and Walkerdine (1982) found in their study of primary mathematics teaching that female teachers of young children often felt threatened and insecure. Infant teachers were also under pressure to justify their approach and this has certainly been part of my experience. I have worked with many women teachers who have undervalued their teaching ability and teachers of younger children have often been seen as having less ability and certainly less status in education. For instance, at one school I was promoted from the infant department to the nursery and found parents offering me sympathetic comments, such as 'Is this where they've put you now!' Unequal promotion prospects at primary level also reinforce the female teacher's lack of self-esteem with far more men in senior management posts.

Another consideration before beginning the research was the sensitivity of the issues and I decided that sharing my child-raising experiences would be an important element. Alison Kelly's (1985) evaluation of secondary school research into gender revealed the difficulty of separating personal and profes-sional issues:

> Many teachers made the link between what we were saying about
> girls in schools and the position of women in their own
> families – as evidenced by the number of anecdotes we were told
> about wives and daughters who were either completely happy in
> their traditional role or had broken into non-traditional fields
> with no trouble at all. We were thus perceived as criticizing
> teachers' personal lives as well as their professional practices.
> (p. 140)

When I have visited schools to discuss or observe curriculum areas, such as mathematics or art, discussion has focused on materials and organization. However, equal opportunity issues have often developed into an examination of early childhood experiences, child-rearing practices and personal lifestyles. The personal cannot be divorced from the professional and reference to one's own experience has an essential role in any meaningful exploration of gender issues. All these considerations were uppermost in my mind when I embarked upon a toy survey and observations of children's use of Lego in four primary schools.

The toy survey

The schools represented different areas of Newcastle and were a mixture of private and local authority housing. The junior school contained a small number of Asian children, otherwise all pupils were white. Staff and parents in the nursery, infant and First schools all referred to the influence of toys on children's behaviour and learning. The general feeling was that the increase in gender-differentiated toys had made boys more aggressive, independent and challenging in their play. In my own teaching experience, male fantasy figures, such as He-Man and Rambo, often triggered play which was boisterous and concerned with violence. The contrast with recent toys designed for girls, such as My Little Pony, was stark. In the infant school I visited on 'Toy Day' the packaging on the toy boxes gave clear messages: 'Sabre-toothed Ogre of Darkness, Spreading fear is his favourite pastime . . .' compared with 'Flutter-ponies bring good luck and fill the air with love'.

...ing play with such toys, I watched groups of girls
...ive groups around Little Ponies and Sindy Dolls.
...d around with frightening figures and Trans-
...ever, the same class, without these toys, took part
...e toy sessions in a very different way. There was far more
cross-sex play and girls, as well as boys, played boisterously with
the wheeled vehicles and large bricks. The sharp differentiation
I had observed earlier was far less obvious. In my present class of
5 and 6 year olds, toys from home seem, in a similar way, to
reinforce stereotyping and limit play possibilities. Staff in the
research schools also referred to the influence of Transformers on
construction skills. One teacher commented:

> Since boys have had Transformers their construction skills have
> increased greatly . . .

In the light of this assumption, that is, that both 'commercial' and
'educational' toys influence young children's behaviour and
increasingly divide girls and boys, I carried out a toy survey. The
survey involved all four schools – a total of 363 girls and 323
boys. In the two nurseries parents were asked to select favourite
toys of their offspring; otherwise children drew or wrote about
their choice.

Both teachers and staff were surprised at the results which,
perhaps not surprisingly, indicated marked differences in the toy
selections of girls and boys. At all stages girls selected dolls and
soft toys as their favourite choices. Nursery and infant boys
predominantly selected cars and construction materials. However, by junior level, the boys had moved into computers and
electronic toys, closely followed by snooker tables. These results
echoed a major mathematics report published in 1982:

> A child-rearing practice which may have an effect on mathemati-
> cal attainment is the fact that boys are given significantly more
> spatial ability developing and scientific toys, rather than the dolls
> which the girls receive. (Cockcroft Report 1982: 280)

Whether children came from a single-sex family or not made
no significant difference to the choices made. One girl in the
survey selected a Transformer and one boy selected a doll (male
of course!). Computer choices were very similar to Straker's
(1985) research which found that three times as many boys as
girls had access to computers at home. In discussion with

teachers and parents it was clear that computers were seen as mainly appealing to boys. In the nursery class staff commented:

> The boys show more interest in the computer than the girls and stay longer – definitely . . .

A father told me:

> My eldest daughter wants a computer, but I thought it was boys who go in for them.

Many of the computer games described by the boys were concerned with warfare, adventure quests and featured male heroes. Mention was also made by boys of their fathers' involvement in computers, construction play and other games such as snooker. No children mentioned playing with their mothers and one girl wrote:

> My dad bought me a train-set because he wants to play with it. I like my dolls.

This toy survey indicated that boys are far more likely to have toys that develop spatial ability and that provide opportunities for problem solving. These boy-preferred toys have educational spin-offs in a way that dolls and soft toys do not. If a girl takes her doll apart she is seen as disturbed! Another toy survey carried out in Havering by Blinko (1986) showed a similarly wide gender differentiation. These results illustrate that girls' avoidance of technology is established in their early years. No wonder Kilkenny's study of Northumberland High Schools found that the craft, design and technology areas emerge as the most strongly sex-stereotyped areas of the curriculum. She argues:

> In a society which is beginning to become increasingly dependent on technology, all pupils need the knowledge and skills to be able to cope with it, otherwise they become dependent on technological experts . . . At present women have too little influence on technological decision-making because they do not know enough about it. (Kilkenny 1985: Appendix 2)

Several infant and nursery teachers told me that they had little knowledge of electrical things and technology. One asked me why her husband 'knew' how to do electrical things when she herself did not have any idea and added, 'Has the metal Meccano disappeared? I was always envious of boys being allowed to play with it, it seemed real somehow . . .' I did come across children who did have metal Meccano at home. However, they were all boys. In the Assessment of Performance Unit's (1986) research into physics, the area where girls consistently obtained lower marks was 'electricity'. The report links this with differentiation in the hobbies and pastimes of young children. Similarly, the GIST (Girls Into Science and Technology) project also found substantial sex differences in the attitudes and interests of 11 year olds. The boys' preference for model-making, construction and building activities afforded them concrete experience of the concepts and phenomena involved in advanced scientific study. In the light of all this evidence, primary schools ought to be considering some sort of programme for girls which would enable them to develop a confidence in the 'science' areas of the curriculum.

In summary, the toy survey revealed that there are pronounced sex-stereotyped differences in the toy choices of young children; that boys are advantaged by play with toys that facilitate scientific and technological understanding and that girls are far less likely to have access to a computer at home. The educational implications of these toy choices were noted by teachers even at nursery level, where Transformers had encouraged construction skills in boys. Both teachers and parents felt that toys developed aggressive, independent behaviour in boys and passivity in girls.

The Lego research

The toy survey confirmed early differentiation in girls' and boys' interests. I therefore decided to look at a 'toy' that is also found in many classrooms and linked to early mathematical and scientific development. This resulted in observing one hundred children between 5 and 9 years of age building with Lego. In the toy survey far more boys than girls had selected Lego as a toy choice at home. My own teaching observations had shown clearly that, if given free choice, by 6 to 7 years of age, boys in classrooms dominated Lego play and girls had lost any initial interest and were often prevented from such play by boys.

I withdrew groups of three or four children and asked them to build a model with Lego, working either alone or with a friend. Three types of Lego were examined. The sample sizes for 1053 and 1030 (Technic) Lego were too small to draw any conclusions apart from the greater proficiency of the boys' constructional skills. The ordinary Lego research involved seventy-four children and showed wide gender-related differences in choice of model, construction skills and approach to the tasks set. In seventeen sessions, 83 per cent of girls built houses, whilst 83 per cent of boys built vehicles. When my own children at home helped me analyse these figures, it was suggested I should change them as nobody would believe they were not invented! The constructions mirrored toy choices and, for the boys, their models subsequently became incorporated into their fantasy play. All boys chose to work independently as they pre-planned their models carefully, quickly and quietly, showing clear task orientation. Even the younger boys would ask how long they would be able to work at their models, one 6 year old stating, 'It will take me about fifty minutes to build my spaceship properly . . .' and it did! Thirty per cent of the girls chose to work in pairs and they saw building as a secondary activity with very little pre-planning and concentration on the task. The girls often changed their minds about their models and made no attempt to incorporate them into their play. Boys also employed what I called 'Lego language' in order to gather the appropriate bricks. They used the studs of the Lego as a guide and would phrase their requests accordingly, for example, a 6-year-old boy asked, 'Has anyone got a six-er?'

After 6 years of age, girls often commented on their own lack of interest in Lego:

7-year-old girl: I used to play with the big Lego when I was little
. . .

6-year-old girl: I've made houses before – they're dead easy . . .

The eight single-sex groups revealed clearly that girls were judged by boys as not being very 'good' at Lego and indeed many girls accepted this evaluation of their abilities:

8-year-old girl: The boys are the best . . . you can say that again!
8-year-old boy: Girls cannot build anything . . . they just laugh, they are silly and play with houses and schools.

At the same time, several girls demonstrated a resentment towards this state of affairs and complained about the boys' behaviour in the classroom:

7-year-old girl: The boys pinch it [the Lego] off me. They use it for the A Team . . . and get wrong off the teacher for making a noise.

7-year-old girl: I like playing but all the boys keep it and don't let us have it. They think girls can't use it.

Another worrying factor that emerged in the single-group sessions was that boys' derisory comments about girls' inexperience with Lego became more marked as children got older. For example:

9-year-old boy: The girls won't want to come and build with Lego . . . they're daft and play with Care Bears.

Boys who did not join in the abuse were taunted and ridiculed for playing with 'girls' toys'. One 8-year-old boy said of another boy in the class, 'He's soft . . . he plays with his sister's Sindy doll.' Similar situations occurred in girl-only groups – a girl who did not participate was mocked for playing with He-Man, to which she responded by going bright red.

So, toys can be, and are, used to reinforce gender conformity. I was not surprised to be told by one mother that her son played with his sister's 'Wendy House' indoors but not outside in the garden for fear of being called a 'cissy'. The Lego sessions which I observed confirmed that gender differentiation certainly does influence the use of the Lego and unless teachers intervene then it is likely that girls' low level of interest and consequent technological underachievement will remain.

To summarize, the main points which emerged from the observation of children's play with Lego were very similar to those found in the toy survey. The models children chose to build were sex stereotypical with girls building houses and boys constructing vehicles which moved. The Lego play showed that boys appear to be more task-orientated, have developed superior construction skills and pre-plan models independently by 6 to 7 years of age. Girls, however, see Lego as mainly for boys, their models are more simple in design and are not incorporated into fantasy play. They appear to gain little satisfaction from such activities. Finally, as children move from 5 to 9 years of age the separation of girls and boys becomes more evident and members of the opposite sex are frequently ridiculed in peer group play if they do not conform to gender expectations.

Conclusion

This examination of children's early play patterns at home and at school showed clearly that girls are disadvantaged at an early age. Attitudes that are developed at primary level ensure that by secondary school girls undervalue their abilities and under-achieve in physics, maths, computer studies and technology. Boys are able to obtain more teacher time and monopolize certain materials in many classrooms. The educational spin-offs of these behaviour patterns must be spelt out to teachers and parents. Unless they are given evidence of this imbalance, how can they be expected to try and redress it? Material by the Equal Opportunities Commission and the Genderwatch pack together with recent maths and physics reports (mentioned earlier) are important back-ups and help explain the reasons for concern. I would also recommend teachers to carry out simple research in their own schools to motivate and inform staff about what is happening in their own particular institution. For instance, I found the materials from the toy survey were very useful in parental and staff discussions. We tried to avoid allowing these discussions to become side-tracked into political arguments. Instead, the importance of widening all children's educational opportunities was the factor stressed.

My research indicated that very young children are well aware of gender 'rules' and they often welcomed the opportunity to openly discuss and sometimes challenge them. Children could easily carry out surveys of school life (playground behaviour for example) and reflect upon them. However, it is for individual schools to draw up action plans which cover all aspects of gender discrimination in primary schooling. In one school I visited, staff had several meetings focusing on language and the 'gender messages' inherent in it. When a supply teacher arrived and started asking for 'strong boys' and 'well-mannered little girls', the staff realized how far their own understanding had increased. Teachers traditionally have used these terms to praise children and so have unfortunately contributed towards society's stereo-typing, thus limiting a child's potential from an early age. In another school, older boys were encouraged to work in the nursery in order to develop the caring role that staff felt they lacked. I met teachers that informally monitored each other in the classroom to see if they could alter boys' dominance of their

time. Once teachers realize the situation they can try out a
variety of strategies which challenge gender differentiation, such
as girl-only sessions for Lego and computer work. Yet, it is
providing the opportunity for teachers to consider gender issues
that has to be the first priority. All Newcastle schools have been
directed to hold a Baker Day concerned with gender. These
training days are run by women teachers rather than advisers. I
am part of a team of three teachers and the sessions I have been
involved in are proving an exciting way forward. When women
practitioners themselves become involved in training, the shared
teaching experiences mean that issues can be explored in more
depth with the teacher/expert situation being replaced by colleagues enabling each other to look at classroom practice. These
training sessions have allowed me to disseminate research findings in a way that is accessible to classroom teachers. Boys
demanding teachers' attention and their disruptive behaviour are
particularly commented upon! I have found that most teachers
have generally no knowledge of gender research. However,
when the teachers can be actively encouraged to become
involved in research and discuss their findings with colleagues
then curricular changes may be attempted. It seems to me to be
far more productive to say to a teacher, 'What have you found?'
than to say 'Do this . . . do *not* do that.' I have read many
guidelines for good practice but often they do not allow or invite
teachers to explore the reasons why. Could this be connected to
the issues raised in my introduction, when I referred to the lack
of status given to the female primary teacher? Tackling gender
issues effectively needs to be linked with women teachers gaining
more confidence and becoming aware of their own position in
society.

To see gender differentiation as only affecting girls is to
misunderstand it and to focus in on guidelines for good practice
alone could be counter-productive. Just as many children in my
research were able to analyse gender barriers, so can teachers.
Furthermore, I would argue that until they are encouraged to
do so, the overall impact of Equal Opportunities shall remain
limited.

Appendix 1

Results of questionnaires used in 1986 Equal Opportunities (Gender) Project in Melton area schools.

Questionnaire 1 results
A   Schools new to project (sixty-five staff)
B   Schools re-visited (sixty staff)
DK   Don't Know

			NO %	YES %		DK %
1	Do you expect girls to be more verbal and artistic than boys?	A	79	21		
		B	87	13		
2	Do you expect boys to be more mathematical and scientific than girls?	A	66	34		
		B	75	25		
3	Do you expect girls to be more interested in reading?	A	72	28		
		B	79	21		
4	Do you line up girls and boys separately?	A	72	25		
		B	95	5		
5	Are separate activities planned for boys and girls?	A	35	65	(mainly	
		B	65	35	games)	
6	Do you accept the stereotyping of sex roles presented in published materials without comment?	A	55	40		5
		B	70	30		
7	Are the examples used in teaching mostly male or female?	A	45 male	35 both		20
		B	70 male	10 both		10

			NO %	YES %	DK %
8	Do you undermine girls/women (boys/ men) performing activi- ties predominantly/ traditionally done by the opposite sex?	A	80	8	12
		B	85	10	5
9	Do you think boys and girls behave differently?	A	31	69	
		B	35	65	
10	Are the pictures in displays mostly male or female?	A	30 male	30 both	40
		B	50 male	20 both	10
11	Do you think boys and girls expect to be treated differently?	A	41	59	
		B	62	38	
12	Do you react differently to groups of boys and girls?	A	53	30	17
		B	65	35	
13	Do you show praise and displeasure in the same way towards boys and girls?	A	23	77	
		B	11	89	
14	Do you excuse behaviour in boys you would not tolerate in girls?	A	86	12	2
		B	94	6	
15	Do you punish boys by making them sit with the girls and vice versa?	A	92	8	
		B	100	–	
16	In groups are pupils seated according to their sex?	A	76	24	
		B	96	4	
17	Do you assume traditional roles are played by the pupil's family? 'Ask your mother to make some sandwiches, sew on a button'?	A	50	50	
		B	60	40	
18	Do you make sexist generalizations, e.g. women can never make up their minds?	A	76	24	
		B	85	15	

			NO %	YES %	DK %
19	Do you challenge pupils or colleagues when you hear sexist statements?	A	35	65	
		B	22	78	
20	Do the boys generally do the heavy work, e.g. carrying projectors, moving furniture in your classroom?	A	56	44	
		B	72	28	
21	Do you expect 'technical' help from boys rather than girls, e.g. in operating projectors, tape-recorders, TV sets?	A	63	37	
		B	82	18	
22	Generally, are girls asked to do jobs in the school which could be regarded as 'caring'?	A	55	41	4 both
		B	60	28	12 both
23	Do you make comments to girls about their appearance?	A	52	11	37 (and boys)
		B	20	9	71 (and boys)
24	Do you in a mixed group rarely choose a girl to lead an activity?	A	85	5	10
		B	100	–	
25	Do you ever say 'Boys shouldn't hit girls'?	A	24	48	28 (both)
		B	58	31	11 (both)
26	Do you show that you regard tears from a boy as wrong?	A	89	2	9
		B	100	–	
27	Do you ever say 'Ladies don't talk/behave that way'?	A	73	23	4 (both)
		B	67	13	20 (both)
28	Do you ever say 'Ladies before gentlemen'?	A	32	52	16
		B	55	40	5
29	Do you consider that there are jobs in your school that are best done by a teacher of a specific sex?	A	42	37	21
		B	68	27	4

		NO	YES	DK
		%	%	%
30 Do you think it is	A	8	78	14
important for children's	B	3	89	8
future aspirations to
see men and women in
senior positions in
school?

Questionnaire 2 Results
Equal Opportunities (Gender) – A Follow-Up Questionnaire

Eight schools submitted returns of the questionnaire which asked the following:

1 *Has your attitude concerning opportunities for boys and girls changed since the initial project?*
   All eight schools maintained they had.

2 *How are you thinking differently?*
   . . . where in the past I wouldn't have given equal opportunities a thought, in the notion it was a problem – much more thoughtful about what's happening in school . . .

   . . . I do question the areas itemized below more closely in relation to Equal Opportunities and take every opportunity to discuss the issues with members of the teaching, non-teaching staff and Governors . . .

   . . . Very much aware of the need for Equal Opportunities in all aspects of school life . . .

   . . . I am much more aware of sex-stereotyped roles and attitudes and discuss them with children, staff, parents and governors . . .

3 *Have any of the following aspects of school life changed since the initial project?*

Organization	six schools responded positively
Curriculum	seven " " "
Hidden Curriculum	eight " " "
Resources	eight " " "
Role Models	four " " "

4   *Please give details of any changes:*
    . . . Concern about hidden curriculum led to displaying different role models from EOC. Slotting in of different maths cards. Eye opening appreciation of the problem!
    . . . Overtly discourage staff from grouping on sex grounds. Have encouraged female members of staff to undertake more science type topics. Have directed my own class more positively so that groupings activities and roles do not emphasize stereotyped models . . .

    . . . Mixed Needlework Lessons. Mixed Maytime Dancing teams. Examination of reading schemes. General consideration of the way that everyone treats the children . . .

    . . . We have mixed registers now and also allow girls to put PE apparatus away. Some of the more obnoxious reading books have been dispensed with . . .

5   *Where do you feel you ought to be in 12 months time in relation to your own school's equal opportunities policy?*
    . . . I hope to have formulated a policy and be looking at other areas of concern . . .
    . . . Further changing of attitudes – both staff and children. One new reading scheme in use . . .
    . . . Would hope for a stronger stance by staff in arguing the need for deliberate and planned action . . .
    . . . I would hope to have discussed the main issues with staff, parents and governors and prepared an equal opportunities policy statement on gender and multi-cultural issues . . .

6   *What areas of change do you feel are still needed?*
    . . . Parents', Governors' attitudes . . .
    . . . Not sure about this . . .
    . . . As a staff we need to examine curriculum materials in greater depth and change them if necessary . . .
    . . . I feel a change of attitude by society generally and I'm not sure how best to tackle this . . .

Appendix 2: Resources

CISSY
Campaign to Impede Sex Stereotyping in the Young
c/o F. Cotton
177 Gleneldon Road
London SW16
(Amongst other materials they produce a bibliography and non-sexist picture books).

Children's Book Bulletin
4 Aldebert Terrace
London SW8 1BH
(Bulletins providing news and reviews of non-sexist children's books)

Equal Opportunities Commission, Overseas House, Quay Street, Manchester. *We Can Do It Now* (a guide to good practice in provision of equal opportunities in primary and secondary education)

Letterbox Library
5 Bradbury Street
London N16 8JN
(Book club specializing in non-sexist and multicultural books for children).

Sex Stereotyping Explored Through Drama
K. Joyce
Teachers Centre
137 Barlow Moor Road
West Didsbury
Manchester M20 8PW

World Studies Activities:
Fisher, S. and Hicks, D. (1985) *World Studies 8–13. A Teachers' Handbook*, Edinburgh, Oliver and Boyd.

Fyson, N. (1984) *The Development Puzzle*, London, Hodder and Stoughton.

Theme work approaches for teaching with a Global perspective: *Development Education in the Primary School*, Development Education Centre, Selly Oak Colleges, Birmingham.

The World Studies Journal, (1986), Vol 5, No 2 (for ideas concerning learning processes). Available from the World Studies Teacher Training Centre, University of York, Heslington Road, York Y01 5DD.

References

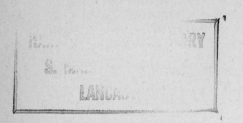

Acker, S. (1986) 'What feminists want from education', in Hartnett, O. and Naish, M. (eds) *Education and Society Today*, Lewes, Falmer.

Acker, S. (1987) 'Primary school teaching as an occupation', in Delamont, S. (ed) *The Primary School Teacher*, Lewes, Falmer.

Alexander, R. (1984) *Primary Teaching*, London, Holt, Rinehart and Winston.

Arnot, M. (1987) 'Political lip-service or radical reform? Central government responses to sex equality as a policy issue', in Arnot, M. and Weiner, G. (eds) *Gender and the Politics of Schooling*, London, Hutchinson.

Assessment of Performance Unit (1982) *Mathematical Development, Primary Survey Report No. 3*, London, HMSO.

Bailey, A. (1988) 'Sex-stereotyping in primary school mathematics schemes', *Research in Education*, 39.

Ball, S.J. and Goodson, I.F. (1985) (eds) *Teachers' Lives and Careers*, Lewes, Falmer.

Best, D.I., Williams, J.E., Cloud, J.M., Davis, S.W., Robertson, L.S., Edwards, J.R., Giles, H. and Fowles, J. (1977) 'Development of sex trait stereotypes among young children in the United States, England and Ireland', *Child Development*, 48, 1375–84.

Blinko, J. (1986) 'Calculated play', *The Times Educational Supplement*, 25 August.

Brah, A. and Deem, R. (1986) 'Towards anti-sexist and anti-racist schooling', *Critical Social Policy*, 16, 66–70.

Britzman, D.P. (1986) 'Cultural myths in the making of a teacher: Biography and social structure in teacher education', *Harvard Educational Review*, 56, 4, 442–56.

Bruner, J. (1960) *The Process of Education*, New York, Vintage Books.

Buchan, L. (1980) 'It's a good job for a girl', in Spender, D. and Sarah, E. (eds) *Learning to Lose*, London, The Women's Press.

Burgess, H. (1986) 'Doubting Thomas: the primary curriculum and classroom practice', *Journal of Education Policy*, 1, 1, 85–99.

Burgess, H. (1988) 'Perceptions of the primary and middle school curriculum', in Carrington, B. and Troyna, B. (eds) *Children and Controversial Issues*, Lewes, Falmer.

Burgess, R.G. (1988) 'Points and Posts', in Green, T. and Ball, S.J. (eds) *Inequality and Comprehensive Education*, London, Croom Helm.

Byrne, E. (1978) *Women and Education*, London, Tavistock.

Campbell, R. and Lawton D. (1970) 'How children see society', *New Society*, 19 November.

Carrington, B. and Short, G. (1989) *Race and the Primary School: Theory into Practice*, Windsor, NFER/Nelson.

Carrington, B. and Troyna, B. (1988) (eds) *Children and Controversial Issues*, Lewes, Falmer.

Clarricoates, K. (1978) 'Dinosaurs in the classroom: a re-examination of some aspects of the "hidden curriculum" in primary schools', *Women's Studies International Quarterly*, 1, 4, 353–64.

Clarricoates, K. (1980) 'The importance of being Ernest . . . Emma . . . Tom . . . Jane', in Deem, R. (ed) *Schooling for Women's Work*, London, Routledge and Kegan Paul.

CACE (1967) *Children and their Primary Schools*, A report of the Central Advisory Council for Education, 1, London, HMSO.

Cockcroft Report (1982) *Mathematics Counts*, London, HMSO.

Council for the Accreditation of Teacher Education (1985) *Catenote 1: The Council's Approach to Accreditation*, London, CATE.

Council for National Academic Awards (1980) *Sex Discrimination and the Equality of Opportunity*, London, CNAA/EOC.

Croll, P. (1985) 'Teacher interaction with individual male and female pupils in junior-age classrooms', *Educational Research*, 27, 3, 220–23.

Dale, R., Esland, G., Fergusson, R. and MacDonald, M. (1981) *Politics, Patriarchy and Practice*, Lewes, Falmer.

Damon, W. (1977) *The Social World of the Child*, San Francisco, Jossey-Bass.

Deem, R. (1978) *Women and Schooling*, London, Routledge and Kegan Paul.

Delamont, S. (1980) *Sex Roles and the School*, London, Methuen.

Delamont, S. (1983) 'The conservative school? Sex roles at home, at work and at school', in Walker, S. and Barton, L. (eds) *Gender, Class and Education*, Lewes, Falmer.

Denscombe, M. (1982) 'The "hidden pedagogy" and its implications for teacher training', *British Journal of Sociology of Education*, 3, 3, 249–65.

DES (1976) *Sex Discrimination Act 1975*, Circular 2/76. London, HMSO.

DES (1982) *The New Teacher in School*, London, HMSO.

DES (1983) *Teaching Quality*, London, HMSO.

DES (1987a) *Statistics of Education, Vol. 10, School Leavers CSE and GCE 1987*, London, HMSO.

DES (1987b) *The National Curriculum Consultative Document*, London, HMSO.

DES (1987c) *Quality in Schools: the Initial Training of Teachers*, London, HMSO.

DES (1988) *Science for Ages 5–16*
Maths for Ages 5–16
English for Ages 5–11
London, HMSO

Evans, T. (1982) 'Being and becoming: teachers' perceptions of sex-roles and actions toward their male and female pupils', *British Journal of Sociology of Education*, 3, 2, 127–143.

Everley, B. (1983) 'Measures to reduce sex role stereotyping in the primary school', *NUT Primary Educational Review: Girls and Boys in Primary Classrooms*, 17, 13–15.

Everley, B. (1985) 'Sexism and the implications for teacher training', *School Organization*, 5, 1, 59–68.

Evetts, J. (1989) 'Women and promotion in primary education. The career and family strategies of married women headteachers', in Burgess, H. (ed) *Teaching in the Primary School: Careers, Roles and Curricula*, London, Routledge.

Fagot, B.I. (1985) 'Beyond the reinforcement principle: another step toward understanding sex role development', *Developmental Psychology*, 26, 6, 129–35.

France, P. (1986) 'The beginnings of sex stereotyping', in Browne, N. and France, P. (eds) *Untying the Apron Strings*, Milton Keynes, Open University Press.

French, J. and French, P. (1984) 'Gender imbalances in the primary classroom', *Educational Research*, 26, 2, 127–36.

French, J. and French, P. (1986) *Gender Imbalances in Infant School Classroom Interaction*, Manchester, Equal Opportunities Commission.

Gaine, C. (1987) *No Problem Here: A Practical Approach to Education and 'Race' in White Schools*, London, Hutchinson.

Gibbs, J.D. (1986) *Equal Opportunities (Gender): A Project in Melton Area Schools*, Leicestershire County Council.

GIST (1984) *Girls Into Science and Technology*, University of Manchester.

Gray, H. (1987) 'Gender considerations in school management: masculine and feminine leadership styles', *School Organization*, 7, 3, 297–302.

Greene, G. (1971) *A Sort of Life*, Harmondsworth, Penguin.

Griffin, C. (1985) *Typical Girls?*, London, Routledge and Kegan Paul.

Griffiths, G. (1986) *Teacher Research: Some Questions, Reflections and Speculations*. Unpublished MEd thesis, Sunderland Polytechnic.

Hanson, J. (1987) *Equality Issues, Permeation and a PGCE Programme*, Unpublished MEd dissertation, University of Sheffield.

Hanson, D. and Herrington, M. (1976) *From College to Classroom: The Probationary Year*, London, Routledge and Kegan Paul.

Horbury, A. (forthcoming) *The Institutional Nature of Pupil Socialisation in the Primary School: An Ethnographic Study*, PhD thesis, University of York.

Hough, J. (1983) *Deprivation of Necessary Skills*, Manchester, Equal Opportunities Commission.

Hough, J. (1985) 'Developing individuals rather than boys and girls', *School Organization*, 5, 1, 17–25.

House of Commons (1986) *Achievement in Primary Schools*, Third report from the Education, Science and Arts Committee, 1, London, HMSO.

Hughes, M. (1986) *Children Understanding Number*, London, Fontana.

ILEA (1985) *Improving Primary Schools*, Report of the Committee on Primary Education ILEA.

Jacklin, C.N. (1983) 'Boys and girls entering school', in Marland, M. (ed) *Sex Differentiation and Schooling*, London, Heinemann.

Jayne, E. (1987) 'A case study of implementing equal opportunities: sex equity', *Journal of Education for Teaching*, 13, 2, 155–62.

Jenkins, R. (1986) *Racism and Recruitment*, Cambridge, Cambridge University Press.

Johnson, S. and Murphy, P. (1986) *Girls and Physics*. APU Occasional Paper, 4. London, HMSO.

Kant, L. (1987) 'National curriculum: notionally equal?' *NUT Education Review*, 1, 2, 41–44.

Kelly, A. (1982) 'Why girls don't do science', *New Scientist*, 20 May.

Kelly, A. (1985) 'Changing schools and changing society', in Arnot, M. (ed) *Race and Gender*, Oxford, Pergamon.

Kelly, E. (1981) Socialization in partriarchal society, in Kelly, A. (ed) *The Missing Half*. Manchester, Manchester University Press.

Kilkenny, M. (1985) *Sex Differentiation in the High School Curriculum in Northumberland 1982–85*, Northumberland LEA.

King, R. (1978) *All Things Bright and Beautiful*, Chichester, John Wiley.

Kohlberg, L. (1966) 'A cognitive-development analysis of children's sex-role concepts and attitudes', in Macoby, E. (ed) *The Development of Sex Differences*, Stanford, California, Stanford University Press.

Lee, J. (1987) 'Pride and prejudice: Teachers, class and an inner city infants school', in Lawn, M. and Grace, G. (eds) *Teachers: The Culture and Politics of Work*, Lewes, Falmer.

Livesley, W. and Bromley, D. (1973) *Person Perception in Childhood and Adolescence*, Chichester, Wiley.

Lobban, G. (1978) 'The influence of the school on sex-role stereo-typing', in Chetwynd, J. and Hartnett, O. (eds) *The Sex-Role System*, London, Routledge and Kegan Paul.

Macoby, E. and Jacklin, C.N. (1974) *The Psychology of Sex Differences*, Stanford, California, Stanford University Press.

Measor, L. (1985) 'Critical incidents in the classroom: identities, choices and careers', in Ball, S.J. and Goodson, I.F. (eds) *Teachers' Lives and Careers*, Lewes, Falmer.

Meyer, B. (1980) 'The development of girls' sex role attitudes', *Child Development*, 51, 508–14.

Morgan, V. and Dunn, S. (1988) 'Chameleons in the classroom: visible and invisible children in nursery and infant classrooms', *Educational Review*, 40, 1, 3–12.

Myers, K. (1987) *Genderwatch*, Self-Assessment Schedules for Use in Schools, London, SCDC Publications.

National Curriculum Council (1988) *Mathematics in the National Curriculum; Science in the National Curriculum*, Epsom, NCC.

Nias, J. (1985) 'Reference groups in primary teaching: talking, listening and identity', in Ball, S.J. and Goodson, I.F. (eds) *Teachers' Lives and Careers*, Lewes, Falmer.

Nias, J. (1986) 'Putting the authority into curriculum', *Journal of Education Policy*, 1, 1, 73–83.

Nilsen, A.P. (1975) 'Women in children's literature', in Maccia, E.S. *et al.* (eds) *Women and Education*, New York, CC Thomas.

Northam, J. (1982) 'Girls and boys in primary maths books', *Education 3–13*, 10, 1, 11–14.

Ord, F. and Quigley, J. (1985) 'Anti-sexism as good educational practice: what can feminists realistically achieve?', in Weiner, G. (ed) *Just a Bunch of Girls*, Milton Keynes, Open University Press.

Pollard, A. (1985) *The Social World of the Primary School*, London, Holt, Rinehart and Winston.

Pollard, A. (1987) (ed) *Children and their Primary Schools*, Lewes, Falmer.

PRINDEP (1988) *Children in PNP Schools: Defining and Meeting Needs*, Evaluation Report 7, University of Leeds.

Rendel, M. (1985) 'The winning of the Sex Discrimination Act', in Arnot, M. (ed) *Race and Gender*, Oxford, Pergamon.

Scott, M. (1980) 'Teach her a lesson – the sexist curriculum in patri-archal education', in Spender, D. and Sarah, E. (eds) *Learning to Lose*, London, The Women's Press.

Sharp, R. and Green, A. (1975) *Education and Social Control*, London, Routledge and Kegan Paul.

Sharpe, S. (1976) *Just Like a Girl: How Girls Learn to be Women*, Harmondsworth, Penguin.

Sikes, P.J., Measor, L. and Woods, P. (1985) *Teacher Careers: Crises and Continuities*, Lewes, Falmer.

Skelton, C. (1985) *Gender Issues in a PGCE Teacher Training Programme*, Unpublished MA thesis, University of York.

Skelton, C. (1987) 'A study of gender discrimination in a primary programme of teacher training', *Journal of Education for Teaching*, 13, 2, 163–75.

Slabey, R.G. and Frey, K.S. (1975) 'Development of gender constancy and selective attention to same sex models', *Child Development*, 46, 849–56.

Southworth, G. (1989) 'Staff selection: some problems and issues', in Burgess, H. (ed) *Teaching in the Primary School: Careers, Roles and Curricula*, London, Routledge.

Spencer, A. and Podmore, D. (1987) *In a Man's World*, London, Tavistock.

Spender, D. (1982) *Invisible Women*, London, Writers and Readers Publishing Cooperative.

Stanworth, M. (1981) *Gender and Schooling*, London, Hutchinson.

Steedman, C. (1982) *The Tidy House: Little Girls Writing*, London, Virago.

Steedman, C. (1987) 'Prison Houses', in Lawn, M. and Grace, G. (eds) *Teachers: The Culture and Politics of Work*, Lewes, Falmer.

Stones, R. (1983) 'Pour out the cocoa, Janet': Sexism in Children's Books, York, Longman for Schools Council.

Straker, A. (1985) 'Positive steps', *The Times Educational Supplement*, 5 April.

Sutherland, M.B. (1981) *Sex Bias in Education*, Oxford, Blackwell.

Swann, J. and Graddol, D. (1988) 'Gender inequalities in classroom talk', *English in Education*, 22, 1, 48–65.

Sykes, J.B. (1979) (ed) *The Concise Oxford Dictionary*, Oxford, Clarendon.

Taylor, B. (1988) 'Anti-racist education: theory and practice', *New Community*, 14, 3, 481–485.

Taylor, H. (1985) 'INSET for equal opportunities in the London borough of Brent', in Whyte, J. *et al.* (eds) *Girl Friendly Schooling*, London, Methuen.

Thompson, B. (1986) *Gender Issues in a Primary BEd Teacher Training Programme*, Unpublished MA dissertation, University of York.

Tizard, B., Blatchford, P., Burke, J., Farquhar, C. and Plewis, I. (1988) *Young Children at School in the Inner City*, Hove, Lawrence Erlbaum.

Wade, B. (1986) 'A picture of reading', *Educational Review*, 38, 1, 3–9.

Walden, R. and Walkerdine, V. (1982) *Girls and Mathematics: The Early Years*, Bedford Way Paper 8, University of London Institute of Education.

Walker, S. (1983) 'Gender, class and education: a personal view', in Walker, S. and Barton, L. (eds) *Gender, Class and Education*, Lewes, Falmer.

Walum, L.R. (1977) *The Dynamics of Sex and Gender*, New York, Rand McNally.

Weiner, G. (1985) *Just a Bunch of Girls*, Milton Keynes, Open University Press.

Weiner, G. (1986) 'Feminist education and equal opportunities: unity or discord', *British Journal of Sociology of Education*, 7, 3, 265–74.

Wheldall, K. and Merrett, F. (1988) 'Which classroom behaviours do primary school teachers say they find most troublesome?' *Educational Review*, 40, 1, 13–27.

White, J. (1982) 'The primary teacher as servant of the state', in Richards, C. (ed) *New Directions in Primary Education: A Source Book Volume 2*, Lewes, Falmer.

Whyld, J. (1983) (ed) *Sexism in the Secondary Curriculum*, London, Harper and Row.

Whyte, J. (1983a) *Beyond the Wendy House: Sex Role Stereotyping in Primary Schools*, York, Longman.

Whyte, J. (1983b) 'Courses for teachers on sex differences and sex typing', *Journal of Education for Teaching*, 9, 3, 235–48.

Whyte, J. (1986) *Girls in Science and Technology*, London, Routledge and Kegan Paul.

Whyte, J., Deem, R., Kant, L. and Cruickshank, M. (1985) (eds) *Girl Friendly Schooling*, London, Methuen.

Willis, P. (1977) *Learning to Labour*, Farnborough, Saxon House.

Windass, A. (1986) *Positive Gender Practice*, Northumberland, Northumberland LEA.

Wolpe, A. (1988) *Within School Walls*, London, Routledge and Kegan Paul.

Wright, C. (1987) 'Black students – white teachers', in Troyna, B. (ed) *Racial Inequality in Education*, London, Tavistock.

Young, M.F.D. (1971) *Knowledge and Control*, London, Collier-Macmillan.

Index